# Economics and Politics in the Weimar Republic

This is a succinct overview of the turbulent economic history of the Weimar Republic. Theo Balderston, an experienced teacher of economic history to history students, summarises the wealth of recent research on the subject, and presents it in lucid, accessible form. He offers new perspectives on the economic effects of the reparations conflict and of domestic political struggles for postwar inflation and the slump. Controversial analyses of the slow economic growth of the Republic, even in its best years, have implications for the instability or otherwise of its political economy. Recent globalisation and global debt crises throw new light on the foreign debt burden with which Germans saddled themselves in the later 1920s, and the fateful financial crisis of 1931. Theo Balderston explains new analyses of the role of economic policy in worsening the slump and thus paving the way for Hitler.

THEO BALDERSTON is Senior Lecturer in Economic History at the University of Manchester. He has made significant research contributions to Weimar economic history, including *The Origins and Course of the German Economic Crisis 1923–1932* (Berlin, 1993).

# New Studies in Economic and Social History

*Edited for the Economic History Society by*
Maurice Kirby
*Lancaster University*

This series, specially commissioned by the Economic History Society, provides a guide to the current interpretations of the key themes of economic and social history in which advances have recently been made or in which there has been significant debate.

In recent times economic and social history has been one of the most flourishing areas of historical study. This has mirrored the increasing relevance of the economic and social sciences both in a student's choice of career and in forming a society at large more aware of the importance of these issues in their everyday lives. Moreover, specialist interests in business, agricultural and welfare history, for example, have themselves burgeoned and there has been an increased interest in the economic development of the wider world. Stimulating as these scholarly developments have been for the specialist, the rapid advance of the subject and the quantity of new publications make it difficult for the reader to gain an overview of particular topics, let alone the whole field.

*New Studies in Economic and Social History* is intended for students and their teachers. It is designed to introduce them to fresh topics and to enable them to keep abreast of recent writing and debates. All the books in the series are written by a recognised authority in the subject, and the arguments and issues are set out in a critical but unpartisan fashion. The aim of the series is to survey the current state of scholarship, rather than to provide a set of pre-packaged conclusions.

The series has been edited since its inception in 1968 by Professors M. W. Flinn, T. C. Smout and L. A. Clarkson, and is currently edited by Professor Maurice Kirby. From 1968 it was published by Macmillan as *Studies in Economic History*, and after 1974 as *Studies in Economic and Social History*. From 1995, *New Studies in Economic and Social History* has been published on behalf of the Economic History Society by Cambridge University Press. This new series includes some of the titles previously published by Macmillan as well as new titles, and reflects the ongoing development throughout the world of this rich seam of history.

*For a full list of titles in print, please see the end of the book.*

# Economics and Politics in the Weimar Republic

*Prepared for the Economic History Society by*

Theo Balderston
*University of Manchester*

CAMBRIDGE
UNIVERSITY PRESS

CAMBRIDGE UNIVERSITY PRESS
Cambridge, New York, Melbourne, Madrid, Cape Town,
Singapore, São Paulo, Delhi, Tokyo, Mexico City

Cambridge University Press
The Edinburgh Building, Cambridge CB2 8RU, UK

Published in the United States of America by
Cambridge University Press, New York

www.cambridge.org
Information on this title: www.cambridge.org/9780521777605

First published 2002

*A catalogue record for this publication is available from the British Library*

*Library of Congress Cataloguing in Publication data*

ISBN 978-0-521-58375-6 Hardback
ISBN 978-0-521-77760-5 Paperback

# Contents

# Preface

This book reviews a rich literature on the interconnections between the politics, economic policies and the turbulent economic history of the Weimar Republic. Limitations of space restrict the main focus of attention to the economic history, e.g. the economic effects of the Treaty of Versailles, or why the slump was so bad. Converse questions about the effects of inflation on the party-political landscape or of the slump on the vote for Hitler could not be accommodated. However, I believe that what is discussed here can clarify the economic context of the great political issues discussed by those more expert in them.

A good five cohorts of history undergraduates endured earlier versions of these chapters and their reactions were vital to the revision process. I hope that a glossary including explanations of even common economic terms (as well as relevant political information) will remove what in my experience are the most common stumbling blocks to the comprehension of economic history. I am most grateful to Harold James for making helpful comments on the manuscript and for advice on reading. He is, of course, responsible for none of its contents. I am also very grateful to Carl Holtfrerich and Albrecht Ritschl for allowing me to use data they have compiled, both published and unpublished, and to Thomas Ferguson, Peter Temin and Joachim Voth for permitting access to unpublished papers.

# Abbreviations

| | |
|---|---|
| bn | billion, used here to mean one thousand million. |
| DDP | Deutsche Demokratische Partei: see Glossary. |
| DNVP | Deutsch-Nationale Volkspartei: see Glossary. |
| DVP | Deutsche Volkspartei: see Glossary. |
| KPD | Kommunistische Partei Deutschlands: see Glossary. |
| MSPD | Mehrheits Sozialdemokratische Partei Deutschlands: see Glossary. |
| NNP | net national product – equivalent to national income – see Glossary. |
| SPD | Sozialdemokratische Partei Deutschlands: see Glossary. |
| USPD | Unabhängige Sozialdemokratische Partei Deutschlands: see Glossary. |

## Economic History Society

The Economic History Society, which numbers around 3,000 members, publishes the Economic History Review four times a year (free to members) and holds an annual conference. Enquiries about membership should be addressed to the Assistant Secretary, Economic History Society, PO Box 70, Kingswood, Bristol, BS15 5TB. Full-time students may join at special rates.

**New Studies in Economic and Social History**

*Titles in the series available from Cambridge University Press:*

12. M. Collins
*Banks and industrial finance 1800–1939*
ISBN 0 521 55271 0 (hardback) 0 521 55782 8 (paperback)

13. A. Dyer
*Decline and growth in English towns 1400–1640*
ISBN 0 521 55272 9 (hardback) 0 521 55781 X (paperback)

14. R. B. Outhwaite
*Dearth, public policy and social disturbance in England, 1550–1800*
ISBN 0 521 55273 7 (hardback) 0 521 557801 (paperback)

15. M. Sanderson
*Education, economic change and society in England*
ISBN 0 521 55274 5 (hardback) 0 521 55779 8 (paperback)

16. R. D. Anderson
*Universities and elites in Britain since 1800*
ISBN 0 521 55275 3 (hardback) 0 521 55778 X (paperback)

17. C. Heywood
*The development of the French economy, 1700–1914*
ISBN 0 521 55276 1 (hardback) 0 521 55777 1 (paperback)

18. R. A. Houston
*The population history of Britain and Ireland 1500–1750*
ISBN 0 521 55277 X (hardback) 0 521 55776 3 (paperback)

19. A. J. Reid
*Social classes and social relations in Britain 1850–1914*
ISBN 0 521 55278 8 (hardback) 0 521 55775 5 (paperback)

20. R. Woods
*The population of Britain in the nineteenth century*
ISBN 0 521 55279 6 (hardback) 0 521 55774 7 (paperback)

21. T. C. Barker
*The rise and rise of road transport, 1700–1990*
ISBN 0 521 55280 X (hardback) 0 521 55773 9 (paperback)

22. J. Harrison
*The Spanish economy*
ISBN 0 521 55281 8 (hardback) 0 521 55772 0 (paperback)

23. C. Schmitz
*The growth of big business in the United States and Western Europe, 1850–1939*
ISBN 0 521 55282 6 (hardback) 0 521 55771 2 (paperback)

24. R. A. Church
   *The rise and decline of the British motor industry*
   ISBN 0 521 55283 4 (hardback) 0 521 55770 4 (paperback)

25. P. Horn
   *Children's work and welfare, 1780–1880*
   ISBN 0 521 55284 2 (hardback) 0 521 55769 0 (paperback)

26. R. Perren
   *Agriculture in depression, 1870–1940*
   ISBN 0 521 55285 0 (hardback) 0 521 55768 2 (paperback)

27. R. J. Overy
   *The Nazi economic recovery 1932–1938: second edition*
   ISBN 0 521 55286 9 (hardback) 0 521 55767 4 (paperback)

28. S. Cherry
   *Medical services and the hospitals in Britain, 1860–1939*
   ISBN 0 521 57126 X (hardback) 0 521 57784 5 (paperback)

29. D. Edgerton
   *Science, technology and the British industrial 'decline', 1870–1970*
   ISBN 0 521 57127 8 (hardback) 0 521 57778 0 (paperback)

30. C. A. Whatley
   *The Industrial Revolution in Scotland*
   ISBN 0 521 57228 2 (hardback) 0 521 57643 1 (paperback)

31. H. E. Meller
   *Towns, plans and society in modern Britain*
   ISBN 0 521 57227 4 (hardback) 0 521 57644 X (paperback)

32. H. Hendrick
   *Children, childhood and English society, 1880–1990*
   ISBN 0 521 57253 3 (hardback) 0 521 57624 5 (paperback)

33. N. Tranter
   *Sport, economy and society in Britain, 1750–1914*
   ISBN 0 521 57217 7 (hardback) 0 521 57655 5 (paperback)

34. R. W. Davies
   *Soviet economic development from Lenin to Khrushchev*
   ISBN 0 521 62260 3 (hardback) 0 521 62742 7 (paperback)

35. H. V. Bowen
   *War and British society, 1688–1815*
   ISBN 0 521 57226 6 (hardback) 0 521 57645 8 (paperback)

36. M. M. Smith
   *Debating slavery: the antebellum American south*
   ISBN 0 521 57158 8 (hardback) 0 521 57696 2 (paperback)

37.  M. Sanderson
     *Education and economic decline in Britain, 1870 to the 1990s*
     ISBN 0 521 58170 2 (hardback) 0 521 58842 1 (paperback)

38.  V. Berridge
     *Health policy, health and society, 1939 to the 1990s*
     ISBN 0 521 57230 4 (hardback) 0 521 57641 5 (paperback)

39.  M. E. Mate
     *Women in medieval English society*
     ISBN 0 521 58322 5 (hardback) 0 521 58733 6 (paperback)

40.  P. J. Richardson
     *Economic change in China c. 1800–1950*
     ISBN 0 521 58396 9 (hardback) 0 521 63571 3 (paperback)

41.  J. E. Archer
     *Social unrest and popular protest in England, 1780–1840*
     ISBN 0 521 57216 9 (hardback) 0 521 57656 3 (paperback)

42.  K. Morgan
     *Slavery, Atlantic trade and the British economy, 1660–1800*
     ISBN 0 521 58213 X (hardback) 0 521 58814 6 (paperback)

43.  C. W. Chalklin
     *The rise of the English town, 1650–1850*
     ISBN 0 521 66141 2 (hardback) 0 521 66737 2 (paperback)

44.  J. Cohen and G. Federico
     *The growth of the Italian economy, 1820–1960*
     ISBN 0 521 66150 1 (hardback) 0 521 66692 9 (paperback)

45.  T. Balderston
     *Economics and politics in the Weimar Republic*
     ISBN 0 521 58375 6 (hardback) 0 521 77760 7 (paperback)

# 1
# Demobilisation and revolution, 1918–1919

Big historical changes often happen in irregular leaps. Such a leap occurred during the months from September 1918, when the German High Command recognised that its war effort had collapsed, and the summer of 1919. During this time the institutions embodying politico-economic power relations in Germany were in flux, and the shape in which to set them was violently contested by opposing forces. The contest was resolved in a matter of months, partly by the forcible suppression of forces on the far left, partly by deals and compromises between the moderate left and the bourgeois centre-right. The voice of the conservative right was little heard in this period. These deals were driven by the short-run anxieties and strategies of the time, chief among them uncertainty about the peace treaty and fears of a bolshevik revolution. These resulted in the political strategies that sought to maximise the chances of encouraging Allied leniency and to strengthen the moderate left. These two strategies came together because it was believed that the Allies, and US President Wilson in particular, would welcome extreme governments of neither left nor right. Germany became a parliamentary democracy with a 'welfare capitalist' political economy – in which private enterprise was morally legitimated by welfare measures and strengthened rights of labour.

But once the left had been quelled – essentially in the first three months of 1919 – and the Versailles 'Diktat' in May 1919 had dashed German hopes of a peace they considered 'moderate', political strategies changed. The business consensus immediately began to regret the compromises made with the moderate left, and the conservative right began to revive. Germany as a whole shifted markedly to the right between the National Constitutional Assembly elections

of 19 January 1919 and the **Reichstag**[1] elections of 6 June 1920.
Weimar's 'welfare capitalism' may appear bland to early twenty-
first-century European eyes but it offended powerful forces at the
heart of capitalism and on the political right, and alienated huge
numbers of workers on the left. To both it remained an object of
bitter contest.

Moreover, as chapter 2 will show, the events of 1919 also saddled
Germany with a reparations regime that Allied disunity thereafter
permitted her constantly to try to revise. Internally and externally,
then, the main politico-economic 'fixtures' of 1919 were contestable
for the rest of the Republic's short history. The uncertainties of
this state of affairs affected the credibility of economic policy. In
the atomised financial markets, the external political disequilibrium
gave rise to huge, shifting waves of speculation. In the politicised
labour market the internal disequilibrium rigidified the opposing
fronts, as each side feared that any slight concession might have
incalculable consequences.

This short book is about the interaction of economic policy and
market calculation, in the context of these political uncertainties, in
shaping the economic history of the Weimar Republic. This chapter
is particularly about the economic consequences of the internal
political convulsions of post-defeat Germany.

It is hard to understand the complex, contradictory character of
'the German revolution' without reading an authoritative narrative
(Ryder, 1967; Carsten, 1972; Kolb, 1988). Here only some of the
main strands can be identified:

- There was a revolution from above. When the Army High Command foresaw the inevitability of defeat in September 1918, it
  demanded the appointment of a parliamentary government, in order to placate President Wilson's preference for negotiating with
  a democratic Germany. A government formed by the Reichstag
  parties and requiring legislative sanction not merely for its domestic civilian policies (this was already mainly the case in the
  **Kaiserreich**) but also for its foreign and defence policies, was a
  novelty in Germany.
- On the other side, since mid-1917 the liberal parties, the (Catholic)
  **Centre Party**, and the more right-wing socialist **MSPD** had

---

[1] Words in bold show the first occurrences of terms explained in the Glossary.

exerted a growing *parliamentary* claim on power 'from below'. In October 1918 leaders of these parties joined the last imperial cabinet under Prince Max von Baden.

- The war had also strengthened organised labour. Before the war **trade unions**, despite a membership of about 3 million, had enjoyed little official or workplace recognition. Collective wage negotiation was the exception, not the rule, except in some south German trades. During the war, the military's short-term interests in production had taken precedence over the entrepreneurs' interest in a workplace regime for maximising long-run profits; and a tacit alliance between the State and the unions had set up machinery, involving the unions, for controlling wartime wage-setting and other conditions of employment (Feldman, 1966). The unions had an interest in perpetuating these wartime gains.

- War weariness had proved a hospitable culture for left-wing socialist agitation on behalf of socialist revolution, the Russian revolution supplying inspiration. Such socialists operated on the left wing of the **USPD**. Spontaneous protest movements at the beginning of November 1918, starting with a sailors' mutiny in Kiel, sparked a 'Soldiers' and Workers' Councils' movement throughout Germany. Mass demonstrations in Berlin on 9 November led, at last, to the Kaiser's abdication, and to the proclamation of a German Republic by a leading MSPD politician, Philipp Scheidemann (to forestall like action by the USPD left wing). The same day a Council of People's Representatives, consisting of three MSPD and three USPD members was announced as Germany's government under the chairmanship of the MSPD leader Friedrich Ebert, the bourgeois parties having retired to the margins.

- Cutting across these political fronts there was a widespread reaction against the irksomeness and perceived inefficiency and inequity of government controls on consumption, industrial and especially agricultural prices and production, and deployment of labour. The phrase 'compulsion economy' (*Zwangswirtchaft*) expressed this revulsion.

- Yet, contrarily, there was also an emergent, radical right-wing critique of unfettered profit-seeking by business in disregard of 'national' objectives and interests. From our post-Cold-War standpoint of capitalism triumphant, it is hard to recollect the degree to which capitalism was a contested idea before 1914, not just for socialists but for others concerned at the seemingly inexorable trend to monopoly – for Catholic social thinkers, for conservatives opposed to speculation, etc. The successes of the war economy impressed many on the right, too, with its apparent vindication of the superior efficiency of State planning over market anarchy in harnessing national resources to national ends. These 'common economy' (*Gemeinwirtschaft*) theorists, notably Walther Rathenau and W. von Moellendorf, advocated establishing compulory **cartels** of key industries under the direction of boards including representatives of the State and consumers as well as owners, which were to effectuate some sort of moral revolution, and set output and prices at levels serving the public rather than the private good (Maier, 1975, pp. 140–6; Barclay, 1986).

• Amid the swirling currents created by the above forces, professional civil servants in the **Reich** Business Ministry and the Labour Office were trying to work out an orderly demobilisation of troops and the economy, that would minimise disruption to civil peace and production. Their plans involved continued reliance, for the time being, on the extensive wartime apparatus of controls (Feldman, 1970).

The prospect of radical socialism was averted by the astute tactics of the MSPD (which could still count on the overwhelming support of socialist voters). Right from the outset, it had seized the initiative. It was less internally disunited than the USPD whose only real bond of union was opposition to the war. The MSPD was quickly able to set the switchpoints towards a parliamentary republic by fixing elections for a constitutional National Assembly for 19 January 1919. It sidelined calls for **socialisation** of the 'commanding heights' of the economy as early as 18 November by securing the appointment of a 'Socialisation Commission'. Socialisation seemed untimely to the MSPD because it could seriously disrupt production and demobilisation. They could field the argument that socialised industries were more likely to suffer exactions at the hands of the rapacious reparations-seeking Allies. Their earliest 'socialist' measures were welfarist. Worried that demobilisation problems could erode political stability, the new government decreed a general unemployment benefit on 13 November and retained wartime ceilings on rents and prices of necessities, and controls on dismissal of labour. The government established its power on the streets against the radical left by negotiating the support of the Army High Command (the 'Ebert–Groener Pact' of 10 November); and it also managed to dominate the proceedings of an All-German Congress of Soldiers' and Workers' Councils in December. At this stage many workers probably supported the revolution more in order to get rid of a war-mongering autocracy than to overthrow capitalism. The decision of the USPD to leave the Council of People's Representatives at the end of December (its inner disunity would hardly stand the strain of government) eased the MSPD's management of power.

On the other hand the government had to surrender the initiative in the management of economic demobilisation to a surprising shotgun alliance of business and labour leaders, who hastily concluded the so-called Stinnes–Legien Agreement of 15 November 1918. Stinnes was a buccaneering heavy industrialist whose initiative in this matter was supported by a group of other self-selected big-business leaders. Legien was the General Secretary of the Commission of the Free (i.e. Socialist) Trade Unions. Under this agreement business undertook to:

- Negotiate **collective labour contracts** with the unions, covering wages and other conditions of work.
- Reform the (often powerful) employer-controlled recruitment agencies so as to end the blacklisting of union members.
- Stop supporting 'yellow' or 'company unions' and establish works councils in all larger workplaces.
- Concede the eight-hour day – a central demand of unions throughout western Europe since the 1870s. The employers' private reservations – that the implementation of this should be conditional on its introduction throughout the industrial world – were swept aside in the published declaration.

In return for these and some more immediate undertakings, business secured trade-union participation in the *Zentrale Arbeitsgemeinschaft* – the 'Central Co-operating Partnership between Business and Labour' that was to manage the demobilisation process and facilitate co-operative crisis management in industry in the longer run. It was to be supported by a substructure of similar bodies at the industrial and regional/local interfaces between capital and labour, which failed to materialise in the event (Feldman, 1970; Kocka, 1984, pp. 159–61; Bessel, 1993, pp. 103–11; Feldman, 1993, pp. 93–5, 106–12). The government subsequently enacted various points of the Stinnes–Legien Pact as law – notably the eight-hour day. Legislation of January 1920 required firms employing more than fifty persons to arrange election of a works council, with a mandatory workers' director to be appointed to the **supervisory boards** of all larger companies. To the left, the works councils seemed derisory successors to the revolutionary councils of 1918. But they were a significant breach in the 'Master-in-his-own-house' standpoint of the pre-1914 heavy industrialists. Some of these social-policy initiatives were enshrined in the new Weimar constitution as basic rights of labour (Preller, 1978 [1949]).

Many employers, especially from medium and smaller firms, felt rather railroaded by the agreement concluded by Stinnes and his group, but for the moment it stuck. But why did the previously self-assured, autocratic German big-business community concede so much so rapidly? The revolution certainly panicked them into concessions to strengthen the hand of the moderate labour leadership with its rank and file, lest they soon be at the mercy of the Spartakists (proto-Communists). But both business and labour also shared an eagerness to 'get the State off their backs' and manage demobilisation without bureaucratic regulation and interference Already, on 7 November business and labour had jointly persuaded the government of Max von Baden to transfer responsibility for economic demobilisation from the Reich Business Ministry to an independent agency headed by Lieutenant Colonel Joseph Koeth, and to involve labour and capital in the decision-making of this agency. Koeth's strategy was practical and short term: to minimise unemployment during the demobilisation transition. One of the best guarantors of this, he believed, was the promise of profit. To this end he resisted regulatory proposals that threatened business autonomy (Feldman, 1993, pp. 93–5, 109–22).

In fact the double demobilisation – of servicemen and of businesses – proceeded amazingly smoothly, thanks to the silent retraction of women from war employments, to a dose of inflationary demand, to the concessions to capitalist autonomy in the pursuit of profit, and to the moral and legal pressures on employers to hire and keep workers. In the short run the market-based success of demobilisation satisfied returning soldiers and most workers, and this preoccupation with 'making ends meet' shaped the early months, at least, of the revolution (Bessell, 1993). However, in early 1919 the mood changed. In January the MSPD government brutally suppressed an ill-organised proto-Communist uprising in Berlin, with the aid of bands of volunteer ex-officers known as *Freikorps*, and continued forcibly to suppress uprisings and workplace occupations in the Ruhr and elsewhere in the early months of 1919 (Kolb, 1988, pp. 14ff).

The elections of 19 January 1919 left the MSPD and USPD jointly in an unexpected minority, but gave the 'peace coalition' parties of 1917 (MSPD, **DDP**, Centre) a smashing majority. A liberal, parliamentary constitution for the Weimar Republic was hammered out over the next six months. Ambitious plans to give the Reich government centralised control of direct taxation (hitherto direct taxation had been customarily reserved to the federal states) were ultimately realised in autumn 1919 to spring 1920 under the dynamic Centre-Party leader Matthias Erzberger. He introduced a steeply progressive income tax, which, coupled with the wartime turnover tax, became one of the twin pillars of Reich taxation. He also introduced a capital levy, with swingeing rates on larger fortunes, to help meet the enormous national debt problem – a measure discussed in all European ex-belligerents in 1919 but enacted nowhere else (Moulton and McGuire, 1923, pp. 161ff; Feldman, 1993, pp.160–4; inflation subsequently reduced the levy to insignificance). These reforms aroused amazingly little controversy, maybe because of the threat of reparations, maybe because of the contradictory tax interests of war debt-holders and other wealth-holders.

In the spring of 1919 the 'Common Economy' Plans of the right gained the unlikely adherence of the MSPD Reich Labour Minister, Rudolf Wissell. But they came to little against opposition in the rest of the cabinet (Barclay, 1986). Reich Coal and Potash Councils were, however, set up in 1919, and a short-lived 'Iron Industry Federation' was established in March 1920 (Feldman, 1977; 1993, pp. 138–55). In time the Coal and Potash Councils were 'captured' by the owners. A 'provisional' Reich Economic Council was also established, a 'talking shop', supposed to examine economic legislation before its submission to the Reichstag. It provides a rich source for historians of economic policy, but had no teeth.

Anxieties about demobilisation are regarded by Feldman and others as the principal influence on the economic and social policies of the day (Feldman, 1975; 1993, pp. 120f, 126–8). The 'economic order' it established has been judged in two slightly different ways by historians.

Witt (1982b) judged that the 'integrated economic, social and financial policy' of the 1919–20 governments was capable of delivering economic growth, stability and distributional equity, via its employment policy (as witnessed in the demobilisation strategy), welfare and unemployment policy, active promotion of statistical knowledge of the economy (Tooze, 1999), and progressive taxation. But the attempt was subverted by business non-compliance and by tax evasion by wealth-holders, which drove the economy into inflation. However, even if it failed at the time, this experiment pioneered the consensus economic and social policies which have underpinned economic crisis-management in continental western Europe since 1945.

Writing outside the Keynesian tradition, the great Austrian economist Joseph Schumpeter (1939, vol. 2, pp. 714f) reached a less favourable verdict. He concluded that German economic policy in this era simply fell between two stools, being neither capitalist nor socialist. It created a kind of limping capitalism, or 'labourism' which could not deliver prosperity and undermined the attempt of Germany's first republic to legitimise itself. Business found itself saddled with the concessions it had been panicked into in the 'Stinnes–Legien' agreement.

Whichever view is correct, the postwar economic settlement was inherently unstable, always revisable if ever the power-balance that had shaped it shifted. The boldness and diversities of the futures imagined in 1918–19 by the several groups on the left and the right were submerged, but they did not die. Right-wing opposition to the Republic revived with the publication of the Versailles 'Diktat' and assisted the growth of the **DNVP**. Reduction of top marginal direct tax rates, and reintroduction of tariffs, both in 1925, were insufficient to modify their association of the Republic with its revolutionary origins. On the other side, the MSPD's suppressions of left-wing uprisings in 1918–20 alienated many of its supporters and drove an irreparable divide between right- and left-wing socialism. The latter solidified into the anti-republican German Communist

Party. The fierce competition between the two socialist parties at times forced the **SPD** into more anti-capitalist and anti-bourgeois stances than it might otherwise have adopted.

The result was a tense political stalemate because only a coalition of most larger parties other than the **KPD** and the DNVP could command a Reichstag majority. The main problem was the difficulty of including both the SPD and the **DVP** (for short spells in 1925 and 1927 the DNVP joined non-SPD coalitions). The stalemate made one party – the **Centre Party** – a member of all governing coalitions and cabinets of the Republic. The Centre Party consisted of a delicate balance between its business and labour wings. Its own latent inner contradictions embodied, and helped to sustain the 'welfare capitalist' compromise that characterised the Republic (McNeil, 1986, pp. 12ff; Ferguson, 1997, pp. 267–73).

Meanwhile, in the short run, Koeth bought time for capitalism. He had succeeded in 'degrading the revolution to a wage movement' as the 'revolutionary shop steward' Emil Barth had warned in November 1918. This strategy, of securing wage concessions but resisting the political demands of labour, would have spelled rising unemployment but for an accommodatory monetary policy. Koeth's policy was thus one source of the postwar inflation (Ferguson, 1995, pp. 180–97).

## 2
## Treaty, reparations and 'capacity to pay'

The Treaty of Versailles had a huge economic impact on the Weimar Republic. In the early 1920s this impact extended beyond the actual expropriations to the indirect effect of the ongoing 'cold war' between Germany and the Allies on the German **terms of trade**, and on the financial markets' calculations of the stability of the German currency. This chapter provides a summary history of the Treaty and particularly of reparations, and seeks to develop an integrated political and economic framework for analysing the effects. It focuses on the early 1920s. Chapters 4 and 5 include discussions of the effects after 1923.

The Treaty was negotiated between January and May 1919 among the leaders of the 'Allied and Associated Powers' without German participation. It was presented to Germany as a *fait accompli* on 7 May. German counter-proposals that sought to trade smaller territorial and colonial losses for a '100bn goldmark' (gm) reparations offer, were refused, and after a severe German political crisis, the Treaty was signed for the German government on 28 June 1919. (Lentin, 1984; Sharp, 1991).

The Treaty redrew German borders, some of them unconditionally (as in the case of restoring Alsace–Lorraine to France and of part of the eastern border with the reconstituted state of Poland), others on the basis of plebiscites to be conducted (the new border with Denmark and the borders of East Prussia and upper Silesia with Poland). It placed the Saar valley and its coal-mining enterprises under French administration for fifteen years to compensate France for the destruction of French mines in the war zone. It prohibited the union of Germany with the new 'rump' Austria, and took away her former colonies and spheres of influence (in China for example). It allowed Germany only a minimal army (for purposes of border control and internal order) and a minimal navy, and prohibited an air force. Inter-Allied Missions of Control operating in Germany were to ensure compliance with the military terms.

To justify the Allies' reparations demands, the Treaty forced Germany to acknowledge her undivided guilt in causing the war (Article 231). As reparations, Germany had to ratify the Armistice's expropriations of German railway rolling stock, surrender most of her merchant fleet (in compensation for Allied shipping losses), make large deliveries of livestock to restock farms in war zones, accept uncompensated seizure of public property and industrial plant in annexed territories such as Alsace–Lorraine, and sign a postdated blank cheque in respect of future annuities. She also lost tariff autonomy. For five years following ratification of the Treaty, she had to admit the goods of Allied countries on the most favourable tariff terms in her tariff schedule, without any reciprocation by the Allies. Special transitional arrangements were prescribed for duty-free trade between Alsace–Lorraine and the now-Polish districts of eastern Germany and the new Germany (Keynes, 1920, pp. 93–6; *The Treaties of Peace*, 1924, Articles 264–8). Numerous other stipulations, from the arraignment (ultimately futile) of Wilhelm II and unspecified others for war crimes, through clauses regulating the discharge of German prewar foreign debts and disposal of foreign assets, to the delivery of the skull of the Sultan Mkwawa to the British (Article 246), cannot be detailed here. Performance of the whole was to be guaranteed by a military occupation of Germany west of the Rhine, and of three bridgeheads across the Rhine for periods of between five and fifteen years – longer if the Germans failed to comply.

### The economic effects of territorial losses, losses of foreign investment income, and tariff discrimination

Germans argued at the time that the territorial and colonial losses and expropriation of foreign assets crippled the German economy and undermined its **balance of payments**. Innumerable historians have agreed with them. This section will not.

Some immediate economic costs of border changes are easy to see. Even without tariff barriers, cross-border trade carries the added transactions costs associated with dealing in foreign currencies and with perhaps having to recover bad debts in foreign courts. But the employment effects of the new boundaries were two-sided. Supplies formerly obtained from firms in annexed areas were often now switched to firms within Germany's new frontiers; to this extent, the border changes created jobs. The adverse employment effects sprang from short-run supply specificities: not all German firms could quickly find new customers to replace those they had lost. This 'structural' problem was particularly acute in the German rump of Upper Silesia, where the border that the Allies eventually defined in October 1921 (following the March plebiscite) violently split local economic communities. East Prussia, marooned from the rest of the Reich by the 'Polish Corridor', suffered similarly. As a result, these remained structurally depressed regions throughout the lifetime of the Weimar Republic. But overall, border unemployment of this sort was not a heavy economic burden on Germany.

The expropriation of German property abroad, and the messy negotiations about impounded German assets in Allied countries, certainly impoverished their former owners. Private-sector owners were generally compensated out of the public purse, and the burden was passed to the German citizenry as a whole. The loss of foreign investment income obviously reduced Germany's foreign earnings, as did the forfeiture of the German merchant fleet. But the common argument that territorial, property and foreign-investment losses directly weakened the German balance of payments is not correct in this simple form. As to the loss of raw materials, the argument considers only one effect of the border change. For not only was foreign currency now needed to pay, for example, for iron ores formerly obtained from Lorraine; foreign currency was now also being earned by German exports to Alsace–Lorraine, and other former German territories. The real cost of the need to import raw materials formerly obtainable inside German frontiers was created by the tariff barriers which the Allies erected against the exports needed to pay for these imports (Graham, 1930, pp. 17–23). These barriers were serious, but independent of the territorial changes.

But even if it was harder after the war to earn the foreign exchange needed to pay for extra imports of raw materials, and even though Germany did lose foreign **invisible** income, these changes did not of themselves weaken the balance of payments and the mark. The **balance of current transactions** with abroad worsens only when Germans collectively spend in excess of their incomes. This is because, ultimately, the prices of all goods and services sold can be analysed back into someone's income, and so, if Germans collectively spend more than their incomes, they also – more or less – spend more than they collectively produce. Although in certain circumstances this will stimulate domestic production, it will also usually mean that Germans will import more than they export. If Germans collectively spend more than their incomes, they also collectively borrow more than they save. A deficitary balance of current transactions only arises when Germans, collectively, are excess borrowers. Although many of them can borrow domestically, in the end this excess has to be borrowed abroad if Germany is to procure the foreign exchange needed to pay for the import surplus. (The importers do not themselves have to be the foreign borrowers; but they must be able to buy some Germans' borrowed foreign exchange). Foreigners will lend for two reasons. Firstly, with the right level of German interest rates, foreigners will be willing to buy German interest-bearing assets. Secondly, if they think that the international value of the mark will rise in the future, they will be willing to speculate in the purchase of **mark-denominated assets**, paying some Germans foreign currencies to acquire these. But if neither interest rates nor expected exchange-rate appreciation tempt holders of foreign balances to offer them to Germans, then Germans will be unable to collectively finance their deficit with abroad, i.e. their excess spending. Domestic interest rates will simply rise to the point where excess borrowing ceases, or (if the central bank doesn't raise interest rates) their currency will depreciate, and domestic prices rise, to the point where the impoverishment from the rise in prices chokes off excess spending. A country cannot have a deficit on its balance of current transactions with abroad if the rest of the world refuses to lend the means of financing it.

In short, territorial losses, losses of foreign investment income and shipping losses did not in themselves cause a balance of payments deficit and currency depreciation. Rather, it was the failure of Germans to 'cut their coat to suit their cloth' – i.e. to cut their spending commensurately with their income loss, that weakened the currency, coupled with the – varying – reluctance of foreigners to lend the foreign exchange needed to finance the resultant deficit.

Irrespective of balance of payments effects, the loss of raw materials could have impoverished Germany if the loss had worsened the terms of exchange faced by the citizens of the new Germany. The Allies might have sought to hold Germany to ransom over the now-needed imports, by charging monopoly prices for them, as had been envisaged in some Anglo-French schemes for postwar global raw materials controls (Trachtenberg, 1980, pp. 1–27). Keynes foresaw an autarkic Europe which destroyed the formerly integrated coal and steel economy between the Ruhr and Lorraine. But instead the opposite situation materialised. A world took shape in which raw materials were in endemic excess supply, and France, far from being able to hold Germany to ransom for iron ore, was embarrassed to find an outlet for it, since the Ruhr steel men now preferred the higher grade Swedish ores to Lorraine minette. The reduction after the war of the German grain acreage reduced the irrational export subsidy that Germany as a whole had paid to eastern German grain producers since prewar days; and after 1924 grain could be bought on the world market at prices that threatened to bankrupt German farmers. The raw material in most seriously short supply immediately after the war was coal; and France was beholden to Germany for this. Freight rates were low because shipping was globally in excess supply. Thus, the Versailles Treaty directly impoverished the owners of forfeited assets and/or the taxpayers whose incomes were conscripted to compensate them: there were no additional 'balance of payments' effects from territorial losses and foreign property losses as such. Higher foreign tariffs on German goods may have impoverished Germans; but they would have been imposed without the territorial changes.

### The politics of enforcing the Treaty of Versailles

Until the 'London Ultimatum' of May 1921, the main burden of the Versailles Treaty on Germany was the loss of German assets. After the Ultimatum, the main burden became the annuities prescribed under the 'London Schedule of Payments'. But these were paid only for about fifteen months – from May 1921 to August 1922.

Payment resumed in 1924 under the 'Dawes' (1924–9) and 'Young' (1929–32) Plans. Throughout, Germany was also liable to meet occupation costs, which were paid in marks.

The direct budgetary burden of Treaty costs (including occupation costs) in 1920–3 can be estimated at about an average of $5\frac{1}{2}$ per cent of **national income**, though in 1921 this rose to about 8 per cent (Holtfrerich, 1986, p. 149; Webb, 1989, p. 108). Explaining why neither more nor less was paid has been a divisive subject from that day to this. It requires attention to the political dynamics of Treaty enforcement.

Allied Treaty enforcement was crippled from the outset by the US failure to ratify it. In the Treaty negotiations Clemenceau, the French premier, had compromised France's demands for a Rhineland within the French sphere of influence, in order to secure an Anglo-American military guarantee against German aggression (McDougall, 1978, pp. 37–41, 57–67; Soutou, 1998). Britain and the US each opposed French plans for the Rhineland, the former out of 'balance of power' considerations and fear of the spread of bolshevism to Germany, the latter because it offended President Wilson's plans to secure future world peace by a 'League of Nations'. So they offered France instead a guarantee treaty until such times as the signatories considered that the League of Nations offered France sufficient protection; the British treaty to be contingent on ratification of the Franco-US treaty (Keylor, 1978; Sharp, 1991, pp. 112f).

However, President Wilson could not persuade the US Senate to ratify the Versailles Treaty, because its first chapter was the League of Nations Covenant, and particularly because of Article 10 of that chapter, which was thought to empower the League to requisition US troops for fighting aggression anywhere on the globe. There would have been sufficient support in both parties on Capitol Hill to secure a modified ratification of the Covenant, or the French Guarantee Pact. But if Wilson could not have his new, just, international order centring on the League, he was not interested in committing the USA to old-style European defensive alliances. An implicit coalition of Wilsonian indifference and right-wing Republican isolationism defeated the French Treaty (Ambrosius, 1987, pp. 136–250). This coalition destroyed the basis of Clemenceau's strategy at Versailles.

And now the Treaty, its provisions unenforced by US commit-ments, left Germany intact, ringed with internally disunited mini-states, potentially the greatest power in continental Europe, given the collapse of Russia, but actually prevented from adequate defence even of her own borders by the minimal, 100,000-strong profes-sional army which the Treaty allowed her. It left a highly unstable political brew in postwar Europe. The German right knew how to exploit this.

US foreign policy under the Republicans (who held the White House from March 1921 to March 1933) did seek to promote European economic recovery – in the hope that this would assist both European political pacification and the export of the surplus US production of those slump years. But this strategy was pursued on the principle of the 'free hand' – and avoidance of defence com-mitments to European powers (Leffler, 1979, pp. 40–53). Mean-while, the indifference of the other Allies deprived the French of any safeguards besides the international legality of the Treaty, and drove them into an ever more wooden, unbending effort to enforce its terms. This attitude manifested itself especially once Poincaré returned as premier in January 1922.

Before August 1923 (when Gustav Stresemann assumed a responsibility for German foreign policy he was to hold till his death in October 1929), German revisionist strategy centred on the exploitation of differences between the intransigent French and the more accommodating Anglo-Saxons. It centred on reparations. Trachtenberg (1980, p. 122) observes, acutely, that reparations were 'the most difficult part of the Treaty to enforce, and the one where the Allies were most disunited. Germany, therefore, had an interest in focusing resistance on the reparations clauses'.

As with the history of 'the German revolution' so with the his-tory of reparations, there is no substitute for a good narrative of its complex history if one wants to understand it (Bergmann, 1927; Trachtenberg, 1980; Kent, 1989). However, space prevents more than a bald summary here.

The armistice contained clauses that were critical to the sub-sequent history of reparations. These limited Germany's obliga-tion to 'mak[ing] compensation for all damage done to the civilian population of the Allies and their property by the aggression of Germany by land, by sea and from the air', plus large surrenders of

German railway rolling stock (to prevent German remobilisation). The Germans understood the adjective 'civilian' to rule out Allied claims for total war costs. Probably the Allies believed this too in early November 1918. President Wilson was committed to a peace 'without victory'; Lloyd George to his liberal sentiments and the French, to restoration of damage in the war and occupied zones. Throughout the bitter wrangle that followed Germany asserted her moral right to this interpretation, as the basis on which she had voluntarily laid down her arms.

But the preamble in the Armistice to the above demands, inserted at the request of the French, had stated, 'With reservation that any future claims and demands of the Allies and the United States remain unaffected'. Exploiting this loophole, once the European Allies realised the completeness of the German defeat, their financial demands on Germany escalated and extravagant demands for reimbursement of total war costs were made by British and French politicians in late 1918 and early 1919. During the 'coupon' election campaign of November 1918, the British electorate proved highly responsive to demands to 'hang the Kaiser' and 'squeeze Germany till you can hear the pips squeak'.

When the Peace Conference convened in Paris in January 1919, the irresistible force of the European Allies' demands for *Réparation intégrale* (i.e. including war costs) met the initially immovable object of President Wilson's commitment to his pre-Armistice engagements to the Germans (Burnett, 1940; Lentin, 1984; Sharp, 1991). After three months the outcome was a compromise: war pensions were introduced as an element of the *civilian* claim against Germany – thus greatly inflating the allowable total but increasing the British and the dominion share of this at the expense of the French and Belgian – but that total itself was not specified as the Allies could not agree. A Reparations Commission was to establish it by 1 May 1921. If Germany recovered economically, it would amount to at least 100bn goldmarks, payable with interest over thirty years – longer if Germany defaulted (*The Treaties of Peace*, 1924, vol. I, Article 233; Annex II to the Reparations Chapter). By May 1921, Germany was to pay 20bn goldmarks on account in cash, kind and assets. The prefacing of the Reparations Chapter of the Treaty by the 'War Guilt' clause (Article 231) was also a device to placate the French. It forced Germany, in signing the Treaty, to acknowledge moral and legal liability for all Allied war costs, whilst in practice Article 232 required Germany to meet only civilian costs (including pensions) in view of her limited 'capacity to pay'. In this oblique manner both the notorious 'War Guilt' clause and the idea of 'capacity to pay' slid into the Treaty, both with unforeseen consequences.

Keynes (1920, pp. 124, 145) thought that a named sum of 40bn goldmarks (£2bn) would have been 'just and wise'. Following him, most historians have presumed that the reparations demands were beyond Germany's capacity to pay, and blamed them on collective irrationality (Kent, 1989, pp. 1, 141). The powerful force of public anger incited by the huge human and other costs of the war seems capable of explaining why French demands were highest, and US demands lowest. However, since the 1970s, some historians have sought more rational or forward-looking explanations for the French reparations strategy, rather than simple retrospective vindictiveness. Reinvigorated by the opening of the French archives, one group interpreted the extravagance of French reparations demands as (in part) a strategy for perpetuating the Rhineland occupation: the less payable the reparations, the longer the excuse to meddle in Germany's western border and thus control the German security threat (Schuker, 1998). Against this, Trachtenberg (1980) argued that the 'true' French reparations demands were quite realisable, unconnected to French Rhineland policy and directed towards restoration of the war zones. Extravagant demands for reparations were voiced before and in the early stages of the Conference only as a kind of blackmail to persuade the Americans that unless the US wrote down the French war debts, made further loans to France during the postwar transition, and, maybe, prolonged wartime raw materials and shipping controls so as to reduce the cost of these to France, France would have no choice but to ruin Germany in order to revive herself.

Kent (1989, pp. 8–9, 72–7) supports irrationality, however. His elegant **fiscal** explanation is that all the European actors pursued large reparations to allay the bourgeois voters' fright at the prospect of confiscatory taxation to meet their country's huge war debts (but cf. Lentin, 1984; Soutou, 1998, pp. 169f). The interests of new income-tax payers and of the new classes of investor inveigled into buying US government debt in 1917–18 have been blamed for US intransigence regarding Allied war debt repayment in the 1920s – which in turn hardened Franco-British intransigence over German reparations. However, Kent continues, Allied politicians in Europe were concerned with appearance rather than reality, and did not expect the large sums they demanded; instead they hoped by 'demagogic and diversionary' tactics to steer round awkward electoral corners. But the worst corner turned out to be the one they painted themselves into: 'once the indemnity cry had been raised, ... the creditor powers did not dare dispel the illusions they had created'. Such a timidity left the French unable to resist the British (and British Empire) initiative on pensions. Offer (1989) develops a general thesis blaming the reparations clauses on the leverage of the primary producing countries of the world in an era of **primary product** shortages: the British dominions, represented at the conference by W. M. Hughes of Australia, were angry that reparations confined to physical damage gave them nothing.

The result does seem irrational. For example, the clear French intention of 'mobilising' reparations is at odds with the large demands that the French continuously supported, and which made reliable servicing of the 'mobilisation bonds' less likely. Lloyd George's switch to moderacy in May 1919, between the publication and signing of the Treaty, seems incompatible with his continued refusal to name the sum in the Treaty and his support for large claims in 1920 and for the London Plan of May 1921 (Keynes, 1922/1971, pp. 1ff; Sharp, 1991, pp. 98f). US government policy, too, was self-contradictory in its refusal to admit the link between the war debt repayments it demanded of the European Allies and its policy of reducing the burden of reparations on German purchasing power. To the extent that this all-sided irrationality was evident to the financial markets, it would aggravate the uncertainty of reparations forecasting. This had implications for the German inflation (see chapter 3).

Only a very condensed outline of reparations history after May 1919 can be given here (cf. also Maier, 1975, pp. 233–304). The Allies refused to negotiate on the German counter-offer of 100bn goldmarks (non-interest-bearing) of June 1919. However, influential British opinion was already drifting against the Treaty terms, partly steered by the mordant brilliance of Keynes' attack on them in *The Economic Consequence of the Peace*, published in December 1919. Keynes had resigned from the British negotiating team in June.

In his book he argued that the Treaty would devastate Germany and that, without the powerhouse of German prosperity, neither the European, nor ultimately the world, economy could regain its pre-war prosperity; and that British recovery was uniquely dependent on global and German prosperity. The book contributed to the second defeat of the Treaty in the USA (Lentin, 1984, p. 140).

For about eighteen months after publication of the Treaty, little was done on either side towards the fixing of Germany's total reparations liability. At Spa, in July 1920, the Allies finalised the division of reparations among themselves: 52 per cent to France, 22 per cent to Britain, 8 per cent to Belgium, etc. (see Moulton and McGuire, 1923, p. 371; where there is a convenient survey of all reparations proposals to mid-1923). After some dramatic pre-deadline manoeuvring (Bergmann, 1927, pp. 53–68; Trachtenberg, 1980, pp. 99–154, 189–91) the Allies published the Reparations Commission's famous and summary assessment of the German liability on 5 May 1921: 132bn goldmarks (£6.6 bn), bearing 5% interest plus 1% repayment. Of this, 50bn goldmarks was designated 'A' and 'B' Bonds to be serviced forthwith. For the time being, neither interest nor repayment was demanded on the remaining 82bn goldmarks of 'C' Bonds. Germany's liability was to be paid off in annual amounts calculated as 2bn goldmarks plus the value of 26 per cent of German exports (Marks, 1978, p. 236; Kent, 1989, pp. 129–38). Note that the payments were fixed in goldmarks; German inflation did not reduce their '**real**' value.

Another ultimatum, another cabinet crisis, and Germany accepted this 'definitive' settlement of her reparations liability. The hopes they had placed on the new US Republican administration were vain in the short run.

In the precarious new left-of-centre German cabinet the chancellor, the Centre-Party politician Wirth, brought in his political protégé, the industrialist Rathenau, as foreign minister to pursue a policy of 'fulfilment', whose aim was to make a credible effort to pay, and thus demonstrate Germany's 'incapacity to pay'. At the same time, the effort to meet the London Plan to which Germany had subscribed would assist Germany's reintegration into the international community, with the associated political and economic advantages. But a proposed increase in corporation tax and a plan for the 'Assessment of Real Values' – i.e. a further capital levy – got nowhere in the summer of 1921; basically, a weak government was caught in the multiple cross-fire between bourgeois refusal of higher direct taxation, socialist refusal of higher indirect taxation and all-party reluctance to be seen to raise taxes for the Allies. The government's credit was too bad for it to borrow and the idea in the autumn of 1921 of a 'credit action', whereby industry would pledge its credit for the securing of a reparations loan, foundered upon the economic-policy conditions the industrialists, marshalled, as usual, by Stinnes, attached to their offer. These included the privatisation of the inefficient and heavily loss-making national railways – which had been used to soak up demobilisation-period unemployment and were a significant cause of the **budget deficit** – and the abrogation of the eight-hour day (Webb, 1989, pp. 33–7; Mierczejewski, 1999, pp. 54f). Business was evidently gambling that the risk of further damage to export markets from further reparations conflict was worth running if they could secure a labour market regime in their long-run interests. It is probable, too, that the German will to comply diminished once the Allied partition of Upper Silesia was announced in October 1921 (Feldman, 1993, pp. 344–84). With great difficulty the government acquired the foreign exchange to more or less meet the instalments required in 1921. By December 1921, Germany was asking the Reparations Commission for a partial moratorium in 1922.

The Reparations Commission was not convinced of the seriousness of the German effort, especially in the budgetary dimension. Nevertheless, in January 1922 it agreed to reduce Germany's liability for the year to less than one third of what was due under the London Schedule – contingent on German tax increases. But in the same month the more accommodating Briand was replaced as French premier by the more obdurate Poincaré. Allied efforts to secure adequate German budgetary reforms in 1922 were frustrated not so much by German ill-will as by German **hyperinflation**, according to Webb (1989, pp. 32ff; cf. Feldman, 1993, pp. 418–33). The **Reichsbank** was made independent of the government, but did not change its policies; and hopes of a loan for Germany to finance immediate reparations payments were dashed in June 1922, when a committee chaired by the (francophile) leading US investment banker, J. P. Morgan Jr, stated that Germany was not credit-worthy as long as the London Plan of 1921 remained in force. Poincaré, to whom 'execution of the Treaty' was the sole guarantee of a favourable European political order, refused to revise the 1921 Plan. His mind turned increasingly to the seizure of *gages* – actual 'pledges' in the form of German property. The 'Balfour Note' of August 1922, whereby the British government pledged itself to seek no more – but also no less – from its inter-Allied debtors than the US demanded of Britain, may have narrowed Poincaré's room for manoeuvre, as well as souring Anglo-American relations (Trachtenberg, 1980, pp. 221–4, 244–75; Kent, 1989, pp. 188–9).

Germany paid only in IOUs from September 1922 and made it clear that she would demand a total moratorium in 1923, and in November the Wirth government was succeeded by a less fulfilment-orientated cabinet under the Hamburg shipowner Wilhelm Cuno. The British made it clear that they would not support French direct action. But in January 1923, in response to alleged wilful defaults on timber and coal deliveries, French and Belgian troops entered the Ruhr in support of an 'Inter-Allied Mission of Control of Factories and Mines' (MICUM). The German government replied with the declaration of passive resistance, and financed a shutdown of Ruhr mines, steelworks and other major industrial establishments, essentially by paying unemployment benefit. This was the commencement of a contest to see who could hold their breath the longest (Trachtenberg, 1980, pp. 276–82). The French won – but barely. In August the Cuno government was replaced by a 'great coalition' running from the SPD to the DVP and with the DVP leader, Gustav Stresemann as chancellor. On 21 September the utter collapse of the mark and threats to the stability of the Reich in Bavaria and central Germany forced him to call off the passive resistance without any concessions from the French. This seemed to be the hour of Poincaré's triumph; Ruhr industrialists were forced temporarily to reach burdensome *ad hoc* arrangements with the French commanders to finance reparations payments in kind in return for the Reich's promise of subsequent (and ultimately handsome) reimbursement. These were the so-called 'MICUM' agreements. But at the end of October Poincaré accepted a proposal, first publicly suggested ten months earlier by US Secretary of State Hughes, to set up two 'Experts Committees' to review reparations arrangements. ('Expert Committees' allowed of US influence through participation by US private citizens, when Congress would not have permitted official US participation.) Strictly speaking, Poincaré restricted the terms of the more important 'Dawes Committee' to making recommendations on German budgetary reform. But he surrendered control of the reparations process to the Anglo-Saxons – the chairman, Dawes, was a US banker. Perhaps, now that he had the Ruhr as a bargaining chip, he followed the 'Clemenceau doctrine' – that for a durable peace he had to have the Anglo-Saxons on board; certainly the mobilisation of 'reparations loans', in which France was vitally interested, could not be achieved against them. US re-engagement in the Treaty process was vital to the political stabilisation of Europe in the mid-1920s (cf. Link, 1970).

The Dawes Committee published its 'Plan' in April 1924. Its main points were (Moulton and McGuire, 1924; cf. Kindleberger, 1984b, pp. 302f):

- A small **annuity** in 1924, financed by the 'Dawes International Loan', rising to a 'normal' annuity of 2.5bn goldmarks in 1928; an undefined 'prosperity index' could be invoked to raise the annuity thereafter. This annuity schedule was seen as a French victory.
- The annuity would be partly raised out of special levies on the German (state) railways and German industry and partly, but not significantly before June 1927, out of general taxation.
- A new gold standard currency was to be introduced (the reichsmark – in October 1924). The Reichsbank was to be placed under international supervision to make its political independence effective.
- *Collection* was separated from ***transfer***. The German government was responsible for collecting (in marks) the sums due as cash payments and reimbursing (in marks) German suppliers of reparations in kind. The revenues collected for cash payments were to be paid into the mark account in Berlin of a new official, the Agent-General for Reparations. Transferring these into foreign currencies was his responsibility, and he was instructed not to transfer if transfer threatened to weaken the mark. However, the German government was expected to do everything reasonable to facilitate transfer.
- The Agent-General also had the duty of reporting on the strength of German budgetary discipline.

These provisional arrangements replaced the London Schedule of Payments of May 1921, but did not abolish the 132bn goldmark total liability (though cf. Marks, 1978, pp. 246–7).

The Allied governments accepted the Dawes Plan at the London Conference of July–August 1924. The French were weakened through their own exchange-rate crisis. The Plan only squeaked through the German Reichstag because some DNVP members broke ranks to vote for it, maybe under pressure from German industry (Maier, 1975, pp. 484–8; Jacobson, 1989).

German policy under Stresemann remained one of patient, long-run revisionism centring on the mobilisation of Anglo-Saxon support. In the event, the transfer of reparations under the Dawes Plan proved less problematic than expected, because the Plan and the success of the 'Dawes Loan' stimulated a flood of foreign (mainly US) lending to Germany. This provided not only the foreign exchange needed for transfer, but also the means for financing a sizeable **trade deficit**. Nevertheless by 1928 the Agent-General for Reparations (S. Parker Gilbert), came to believe that the growing irresponsibility he detected in German central and local budgetary management could best be cured by definitely fixing Germany's reparations liability and substantially restricting the degree of transfer protection. Following his lead, the US government initiated a proposal for a new 'Experts Committee'. The French hoped that revision in advance of a transfer crisis would best serve the hopes they still had of 'mobilising' their reparations claims. The British and Germans were less keen to reopen the issues but the Germans, at least, hesitated to offend the Americans. They also gambled that the direct interests of US holders of German bonds in seeing reparations reduced (and thus made less of a threat to the servicing (in dollars) of their investments), would defeat the opposing (indirect) interest of US taxpayers in higher reparations receipts by America's war debtors in Europe (McNeil, 1986, pp. 191–5, 202, 219–35).

A new 'Experts Committee', this time including Germans, was convened in Paris in February 1929 under the chairmanship of Owen D. Young. In these negotiations the connection between what France (especially) and Britain demanded of Germany, and their foreign wartime debt liabilities to the US was unmistakable, though the US government still denied it. The Committee's deliberations were nearly derailed at the end of April by the German 'experts' – Hjalmar Schacht, President of the Reichsbank, and Albert Vögler, president of the management board of United Steelworks – who demanded the return of the Polish corridor, new German colonies, and Allied tariff reduction, as *quid pro quo* for Allied reparations demands. The Conference was narrowly saved from breakdown when Schacht himself took fright at the currency crisis his demands provoked, and when the German government, labouring under its own fiscal crisis, pressured him to sign. The Young Plan involved a schedule of annuities of 800m reichsmark (rm) less than those of the 'Dawes Plan' normal year in 1929–30, rising to a peak of 2.43bn reichsmark in 1965, before falling again and terminating in 1988 – when the French war debt payments to the USA were due to end. The US government had supported the US taxpayer at the potential expense of the US bondholder, and Germany's wager on US benignity had flopped. Most of the annuity now became unconditionally transferable and hence available for servicing 'mobilised' reparations bonds. The apparatus of foreign control over reparations and the Reichsbank was abolished, and in subsequent intergovernmental negotiations at The Hague in August 1929 and February 1930 the Allies agreed to evacuate the Rhineland in 1930 – five years ahead of schedule.

The storm that the Young Plan raised in Germany in the autumn of 1929 immediately threw doubt on its 'finality' (Schuker, 1988, pp. 47–53). As the German financial crisis and the US economic slump worsened, President Hoover proposed a one-year moratorium on war debts and reparations on 20 June 1931, and, after a delay, the French agreed to it (Kent, 1989, pp. 335–72). Thereupon, chancellor Brüning spared no effort to get them cancelled within the year and von Papen, his successor, reaped the rewards at Lausanne in June 1932. Here the European Allies and Germany 'fulfilled Washington's nightmare of a debtors' coalition', (Costigliola, 1984, p. 237) as the former agreed effectively to end reparations, and then more or less defaulted on their war debts.

### The economics and politics of 'capacity to pay'

Reparations payment can be thought of as a tax collected from German citizens by the German government acting as the Allies' fiscal agent (cf. Keynes, 1971/1922, pp. 54–5) but a tax lacking the moral legitimation that normally assists collection. Of course German taxpayers would want to evade this tax (Feldman, 1993, pp. 348f), and it was they who elected the German government. Payment would certainly break down unless the Germans were co-erced into, or given sufficient incentive for, paying.

This approach modifies the traditional black-and-white debate rehearsed by the historiography. Debate centred on the London Plan of 1921. Keynes held that its 'Schedule of Annuities' was beyond Germany's capacity, and (accurately) predicted a speedy German default (Keynes, 1977, pp. 25, 235–49). Francophile historians argue that the liability was in practice limited to the 'A' and 'B' bonds, which were within Germany's 'capacity to pay': Germany contrived a fraudulent 'bankruptcy'. The Anglo-Saxon view, for the most part, was that payment was beyond Germany's objective capacity to pay (Felix, 1971a; Marks, 1978, 1998; Feldman, 1998). (Note that the possibility of activating the 'C' bonds would affect the calculations of the financial markets, however.)

'Capacity to pay' must be considered in terms of the total tax burden. This tends to favour the francophiles. It can be calculated that the burden of the 'A' and 'B' bonds, relative to German national income was less than that levied on the British poor (i.e. without an income tax) to service the huge national debt held by the British rich in 1821. It must also be considered in terms of the 'transfer burden' on the balance of payments. The 'London Schedule' annuity represented about 60 per cent of the value of Germany's estimated **visible** exports in 1922. This certainly seems well above the 40 per cent considered the tolerable maximum in the debt crisis of the 1980s (Webb, 1988, pp. 751), and tends to favour the Anglo-Saxon view.

Some economists argued that transfer demanded impossible adjustments of the German economic structure. These 'structuralists' contended that the physical relation between German imports of raw materials and food, for German export industries and workers, on the one hand, and the level of these exports, on the other, made a large **trade surplus** impossible. This theory, which naturally had many German supporters, had its first non-German champion in Keynes (1920, pp. 174–85). His arguments were later developed by some US economists who believed that their inductive study of economic-historical cases disproved the elegant theorems of classical trade theory (Moulton and McGuire, 1923; Moulton, 1925).

On the other side of this debate stood those 'classicals', who contended that, provided the German government sought to defend a fixed exchange rate (they had the **gold standard** in mind), the very act of acquiring the foreign exchange to effect reparations transfer would tend to raise German interest rates, causing domestic deflation and falling German prices in relation to import prices. This would tend to deflect German demand from foreign to home goods and also reduce German demand for all goods by reducing German money incomes relative to import prices. These effects would tend to create the export surplus needed to pay the reparations annuity. Graham argued against the structuralists that enlarging the German export surplus need not involve increasing German manufacturing production, but only reducing the domestic absorption of manufactures. Although the 'classicals' conceded that Allied trade barriers could increase the costs to Germany of creating the trade surplus, they were optimistic that indirect trade, particularly of Germany with eastern Europe and of eastern Europe with the Allies, could ease the process (Taussig, 1920, 33–57; Graham, 1925; though cf. Graham, 1930, pp. 211f).

But this debate, from which sprang the economic theory of international transfer (Machlup, 1966), is not focused on the real historical *explanandum*. The relevant question is not why the London Schedule was not fully carried out, but why it was little more than half-carried out in 1921–2. The transfer burden implied by a half-transfer (30 per cent of visible exports) was by no means outside the range that history has proved possible. Does their miserable performance (from the Allies' standpoint) prove the bad faith of the German government, or were they incapable of paying, even if they chose to?

This question should be considered firstly in relation to taxation. The Reichstag's refusal in 1921 to vote for the necessary tax increases to meet the 'London Schedule of Payments' implicitly bankrupted the government, as revealed by its inability to borrow on its own account the hard currency needed to meet reparations instalments, and the attempt (see above) to use the credit of German business to raise a reparations loan. In 1922 the government's incapacity arose rather because the real value of the revenues from the extra taxation voted for was eroded by inflation.

In 1921 the bankruptcy more probably reflected the mismatch between the objectives of the government and those of the political parties, rather than some dodgy deal between them. The unvarying aim of the government was to win a foreign reparations and stabilisation loan. Persuading the international **capital market** that it was not credit-worthy seems an odd way of working towards that loan. And since a bankrupt government is likely to lose control of events at home too, it is most unlikely that it would have deliberately contrived bankruptcy. As the international negotiating agent of the German Republic, the government wished to establish the Republic's credentials as a parliamentary democracy that acted in good faith towards its international obligations. Among other things, this strategy aimed to win British and US support for Treaty revision. Excepting during the Ruhr crisis of 1923 (and then with some British and US complicity), no German government before Hitler so much as contemplated unilateral abrogation of its international obligations, including reparations. But the priority of the political parties was their reputation with the electorate – the reparations taxpayers – not Germany's reputation with creditors. Only a credible threat of Allied coercion, or the prospect of Allied rewards for paying, could persuade the parties to soften their anti-Allied rhetoric, sink their own deep differences over the fairness of direct as against indirect taxation, and suffer the government's proposed taxes. US withdrawal from the enforcement process and British half-heartedness may have encouraged the German government's Treaty-revision strategy, but they also weakened the credibility of the coercion threat. The main inducement would be that compliance would permit fuller participation in the prosperity of the world economy. Perhaps as long as the rest of the world remained mired in the slump of the early 1920s such an inducement seemed rather faint.

But in 1922 accelerating inflation both weakened party resistance to tax increases and frustrated the revenue-increasing intentions of the new taxes. This effect can only be interpreted in the light of some theory of the causes of the inflation. If one accepts Webb's (1989) expectational theory (see pp. 47ff), then the Allied demands and the German response of 1921 so depressed market expectations of currency stabilisation as to reduce actual real revenues. Thus we may conclude that the interaction between Allied demands, the diverse priorities of the German government and the Reichstag parties, and the financial markets' reactions to these political dynamics, rather than German bad faith, explain why Germany raised no more in taxes than she did in 1921–2.

The counterfactual hypothesis to this argument is that with greater Allied unity, German tax resistance would have lessened. Why, then, was Britain more reluctant than France to receive German tax revenues? This reluctance has diplomatic (balance of power) dimensions. But insofar as it was economic, the issue could be viewed distributionally. All Britons and French would have gained from lower taxes or more generous State services. Against this, all producers of goods competitive with German exports might lose when Germany began to run trading surpluses either to pay reparations or to pay off the loans with which she postponed the reparations burden. Coal was the main case in point. More such producers lived in Britain with its mainly industrial exports, than in France. These were only a minority of British citizens, but the wage-earners among them were organised in powerful unions and were key voters just at a time when the 'mould' of the British party system was being remade (Pugh, 1993).

Turning to the 'transfer' aspects of 'capacity to pay', as a benchmark, we should recall the classical view, that the act of increasing taxes depressed domestic demand and increased the export surplus. But no export surplus was in fact earned in Germany before 1929 (1926 apart). It is simplest to start with the stable price period 1924–9.

In this period large import surpluses plus reparations transfers were financed by a high level of foreign borrowing. As shown above (pp. 13f), net foreign borrowing implies spending in excess of saving by the borrowing economy.[2] Such excess spending could have been the result of a high rate of **investment** spending in post-1924 Germany or of a high level of public spending and public sector deficits; but investment spending was not as high a proportion of German national income as before 1914 and, after 1924, although

---

[2] The fact that gross German foreign borrowing, offset by German 'capital flight' to abroad, exceeded net may also reflect aversion from reichsmark-denominated bonds after the inflation (Balderston, 1986).

municipal deficits and borrowing rose, these were no larger than in Britain at the same time; and Britain was not a net foreign borrower (Balderston, 1993, pp. 250ff). The conclusion, then, is that German private consumption spending was unusually high, and private saving unusually low.

Now it would be very odd for Germans consistently to consume more than they saved, if they really expected their incomes to be reduced for decades to come due to reparations. Such expectations should have caused consumption cutbacks and increased savings rates. The foreign borrowing after 1924 may therefore imply that the noisy German public protests about economic enslavement to the Allies for generations were not matched by their private spending and saving plans. Lack of credibility of the reparations demands for the long run frustrated transfer.

Making similar inferences regarding the era of the inflation is harder. Germany is estimated to have had an import surplus of around 6bn goldmarks between 1919 and 1922. In addition Germany had to purchase approximately 2.5bn goldmarks-worth of foreign currencies to effect reparations transfers, and German individuals and firms purchased about 6.75bn goldmarks-worth of foreign currency assets. This huge excess of foreign currency demanded over that earned by exports was not financed by foreign lending in the ordinary way, but by foreigners purchasing some 15bn goldmarks-worth of mark-denominated deposits and other mark assets, hoping to make speculative gains on the mark's future appreciation (Holtfrerich, 1986, pp. 178, 295; Webb, 1989, p. 91). In the event the mark was annihilated and all the foreign currency spent in acquiring these mark assets was a gift to Germany. However, when the Germans spent the 6bn goldmarks in excess of what they had earned, they must have borrowed (in marks) to do so, and as those who lent must have expected to be repaid, it is reasonable to think that those who borrowed must have expected to repay. But 4bn goldmarks of the import surplus was incurred in 1919 alone. Incomes were very low in 1919, and it is not surprising that Germans borrowed against expected future income increases in that year. The smaller import surplus of 1920–2 may therefore indicate far less optimism than the borrowing of 1924–9. Moreover, as inflation returned in 1921–2, Germans who could not save by acquiring foreign assets had either to purchase shares of uncertain value (p. 56) or real assets, so that the act of saving did not reduce aggregate demand and increase the export surplus. The clearest reason for the transfer difficulties of 1921–2 was that the inflation itself frustrated the classical 'transfer mechanism', so that it had to be effected by the unlikely means of Allied speculation!

Thus, Germany's 'capacity to pay' was a function of the relation between Allied enforcement and German compliance, and of the financial markets' assessments of these. However, it suited most of the reparations players to *maintain* that Germany faced a clear, objective balance-of-payments limit on her 'capacity to pay'. It suited the dominant player – the USA – to have the 'structuralist' arguments of Moulton and McGuire translated into the 'transfer protection clause' of the Dawes Plan, because this clause prevented transfer from exerting a deflationary pressure on Germany's domestic market, and thus defeating the US strategy for German and European recovery (Schuker, 1993, p. 400). The same 'safety valve' suited the British, because it limited the pressure on Germany to produce an export surplus. Keynes 'did not expect to see Mr Lloyd George fighting a general election on the issue of maintaining an Army to compel Germany at the point of the bayonet to undercut British manufactures' (Keynes, 1977, pp. 252f). 'Capacity to pay' was obviously also a formula which legitimised the German attempt to demonstrate incapacity to pay – i.e. the 'fulfilment' policy. The losers were the French, who argued that German 'incapacity' was really German disinclination. But France had already conceded the ground: the compromise formula justifying reparations in Article 232 of the Treaty itself made 'capacity to pay' the yardstick of what Germany should pay (see p. 18).

## The economic effects of reparations

Actual publicly financed reparations expenses were about 7.5bn goldmarks from 1919 to 1922, and approximately 11bn reichsmarks from 1925 to 1932 (Holtfrerich, 1986, pp. 147, 152). These were less, respectively, than the approximately 15bn goldmarks lost by foreigners through failed speculation in the mark in the years 1919–22, and the sums lost by foreigners through the repayment and debt-servicing arrangements they had to make do with after 1931 on the German bonds they had bought and bank deposits they had placed between 1924 and 1930. On this basis Schuker maintains that the USA paid 'reparations to Germany' (Felix, 1971a; Schuker, 1988, pp. 106–19). This – in itself accurate – argument from hindsight neglects the costs to Germany of the process by which it came about, and of the uncertainties and expectations this created. These included:

- The Ruhr crisis itself, with its catastrophic effect on German incomes.
- The effect on the German terms of trade and hence German 'real' incomes. Germany's terms of trade deteriorated in this period (Bresciani-Turroni, 1937, pp. 248–50; although Ferguson, 1998, argues that this disparity ceased in 1922). Many attribute this deterioration simply to the inflation; but where both relative prices of exports and quantities exported fell, the demand-side must be considered the overriding influence (Balderston, 1995a). The conflict over reparations provoked persistent Allied hostility to German goods – both State hostility in the form of tariff discrimination, and popular hostility forcing German exporters to offer what they called 'hate discounts' in order to tempt Allied buyers (Lindenlaub, 1985, p. 112). Laursen and Pedersen (1964, pp. 84, 90) following Graham (1930, p. 270) suggested that the German national income was reduced by more than 5 per cent per annum by the terms-of-trade deterioration. Thus it can be argued that the commercial clauses of the treaty, and popular Allied hostility to German goods, had a much greater effect on German prosperity than the territorial annexations. The reason why this economic hostility survived until 1924, but rapidly decayed thereafter, seems to have been that the Dawes Plan enabled a rapid recovery of German exports to Allied countries, which had collapsed during the postwar years (Balderston, 1993, pp. 82-99; but see Feldman, 1998 and Ferguson, 1998 on problems of export prices and quantities in this period).
- The effect on inflation – to the extent that inflation itself was of net economic cost rather than benefit to Germany (see chapter 3, pp. 53–7).
- Possible effects on interest rates after currency stabilisation in 1923–4. Despite the possibility of transfer protection under the Dawes Plan the competitive claims of reparations payments and

debt servicing on Germany's future foreign exchange earnings probably unsettled the minds of foreign lenders (Ritschl, 1998).

• A possible weakening of German popular support for the liberal international economy and strengthening of support for autarkist economic ideas, due to the adverse effect of the reparations conflict on the terms of trade in the early postwar years.

The vexed question of the relation between reparations policy and Brüning's deflationary policies will be deferred to chapter 5.

# 3
# Inflation, 1918–1923

### The phases of the inflation

This chapter and the next two consider the main economic issues in each of the main periods into which Weimar economic history is conventionally divided:

- inflation: 1918–1923
- 'normalisation': 1923–1928/9
- depression: 1928/9–1933.

This chapter explores the complex question of the inflation.

The inflation is popularly remembered for its final stages, its astronomical prices, its suitcases full of money, etc. (Fergusson, 1975; Guttman and Meehan, 1975). However, its most traumatising effects were caused not by the sheer speed of price rise (to which people can adapt), but rather by its variability and unpredictability (cf. Rowley, 1994). The variability of the inflation can be grasped following Bresciani-Turroni (1937, pp. 25–38), by dividing it into seven phases. These are shown in Table 3.1; the periods are defined with reference to changes in the dollar exchange rate, which were more abrupt than changes in wholesale prices.

Inflation took hold of Germany during the war (phase 1). Already one year after the commencement of hostilities – in July 1915 – wholesale prices were 40 per cent higher than at the end of the peace, and by the end of the war they had approximately doubled. Wartime inflation was not out of line with wartime inflation in all belligerent countries and even Switzerland.

After the armistice, inflation accelerated everywhere, but more so in the defeated countries (phase 2). German inflation accelerated

Table 3.1. The German inflation in seven phases

| Phase/period | Wholesale price level at end of period (1913 = 1) | Price increase or decrease across period (%) | Average monthly rate of change (%) of price | |
| --- | --- | --- | --- | --- |
| | | | wholesale prices | dollar in marks |
| 1. August 1914–November 1918 | 2.34 | 134 | 1.7 | 1.1 |
| 2. November 1918–May 1919 | 2.97 | 27 | 4.1 | 9.5 |
| 3. May 1919–February 1920 | 16.85 | 467 | 21.0 | 25.0 |
| 4. February 1920–May 1921 | 13.08 | −22 | −1.7 | −4.0 |
| 5. May 1921–June 1922 | 70.30 | 438 | 14.0 | 13.5 |
| 6. June 1922–June 1923 | 19385.00 | 27475 | 60.0 | 63.0 |
| 7. June–November 1923 | 725.7 bn | 37.4 m | 32700.0 | 28831.0 |

*Source:* calculated from Holtfrerich (1986), p. 17.

again in the second half of 1919, coincidentally with the publication of the Versailles Treaty in May (phase 3). Then it suddenly stopped in February–March 1920 (phase 4). This coincided with the onset of far sharper deflation in the USA and UK, and also with the final enactment of the Erzberger tax reforms, the failure of the right-wing Kapp-Lüttwitz putsch and the quelling of a left-wing uprising in the Ruhr that sprang from resistance to the putsch – all in March 1920. Although the levels wobbled a bit, wholesale prices were 15 per cent lower in March 1921 than a year earlier.

However, from May 1921, following the Allies' 'Reparations Ultimatum' of that month and, perhaps, following signs of renewed wage pressure earlier in the year, German inflation resumed at rates midway between those of phases 2 and 3 – but tending upwards (phase 5). Now price behaviour in Germany and the new states of eastern Europe (except Czechoslovakia) parted company with the temporary or permanent stabilisations in the rest of Europe and the world. German inflation accelerated into 'hyperinflation' after

June 1922, coincident with the murder of the Foreign Minister and 'fulfilment' strategist Walther Rathenau, and the refusal of the Morgan Committee to recommend a reparations loan for Germany (p. 21). The hyperinflation itself is divided into two phases by Bresciani-Turroni. In the earlier phase (phase 6), prices rose at an average daily rate of 1.6 per cent; between February and April 1923 the Reichsbank had been successfully pegging the exchange rate in an effort to control the costs of passive resistance (cf. the table in Webb, 1989, p. 59). In the final phase of hyperinflation, from July 1923, the average *daily* rate of wholesale price rise shot up to 12 per cent (phase 7).

The relationship between domestic prices (indicated by wholesale prices) and the dollar exchange rate also differed in different phases. During the war exchange-rate depreciation was less than domestic price inflation. The **real exchange rate** rose. But after the war the real exchange rate was lower than in 1913. There was a slight tendency for falls in the real exchange rate to be associated with accelerations of domestic inflation (and conversely) but it was not as strong as contemporaries supposed. In the final months of hyperinflation in autumn 1923, domestic price inflation outstripped the fall in the exchange rate and the German real exchange rate rose (Holtfrerich, 1986, pp. 18–25).

Since the 1970s there has been an exponential growth in articles by monetary economists using the German inflation as a statistical database for testing their theories (Siklos, 1995). Historians justifiably criticise the remoteness of the reasoning from the real history. Yet inflation is a monetary phenomenon which works itself out not in parliamentary legislation or political negotiation, but on markets. Only clear and educated thinking about monetary relations in markets can comprehend it, and this is what economists are trained to do. The next four sections of the chapter will survey the history of explanation of the inflation under four headings. The politics of inflation are then discussed in the light of these, followed by briefer sections surveying economic effects of the inflation and the economics of stabilisation.

## The quantity theory of the German inflation

The most basic theory of the German inflation is the 'quantity theory'. Popularised as 'too much money chasing too few goods', its classic historiographic application to the German inflation was by Bresciani-Turroni (1937). It is basic in the sense that almost all other theories embody somewhere the quantity-theory mechanism but differ in what they identify as the originating cause of the inflation. Therefore, to understand the literature on the inflation one must start by understanding the quantity theory.

The essence of the quantity theory is that the cause of the rising prices in Germany was the increasing **money supply**. Figure 3.1

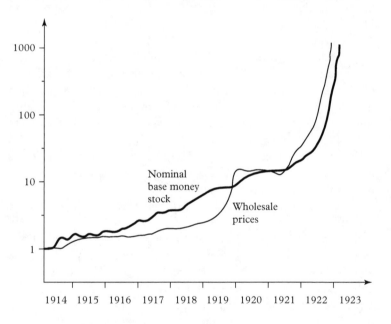

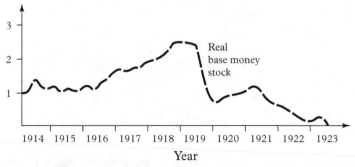

Figure 3.1 Wholesale prices, and nominal and real base money stocks, Germany 1914–23 (1913 = 1), from Holtfrerich, 1986, pp. 17, 52–4.

confirms that the undeflated or 'nominal' money supply rose rapidly. The 'money supply' shown in Figure 3.1 is actually only part of the whole – the so-called '**monetary base**' or the types of **money** that were directly under Reichsbank control. It excluded deposits at commercial banks against which cheques can be written, and in fact grew a bit faster than the entire money supply because of the shrinking importance of bank deposits (Holtfrerich, 1986 pp. 49–63). The supply of **base money** grew primarily because of the German budget deficits and the method of financing these. Both during the war and throughout the postwar quinquennium the government paid only a fraction of the expenses of the state out of taxation and financed the greater part by borrowing. However, government borrowing did not of itself increase the money supply. This increase occurred because the government borrowed some of the funds needed to cover the excess of its spending over its revenues from the Reichsbank – rather than from private-sector lenders on the capital market. This happened because the level of (**nominal**) interest rates offered on State debt was never high enough to entice the private sector to acquire all of it as an investment. Therefore the State had to borrow the residue from the Reichsbank by selling it **treasury bills**. The Reichsbank paid for these by crediting the government's Reichsbank account with deposits and, as these deposits were transferred to private firms and citizens in whose favour the State wrote cheques, the money supply possessed by German banks, firms and individuals increased.

Some of these transferred deposits would be cashed as Reichsbank notes. Before the war, the Reichsbank's expansion of its note issue was limited by the types of asset required to be held as a reserve against it. The Reichsbank had had to hold gold to the value of one-third of the note issue, and good **trade bills** to the other two-thirds. But during the war these stipulations were relaxed and subverted in a manner lucidly described by Holtfrerich (1986, pp. 114f). From now on regulations regarding the 'backing' of the note issue no longer checked the Reichsbank's purchase of treasury bills, because these were, directly or indirectly, the required 'backing'.

Why did an increasing money supply raise prices? If Germany were at full employment, the excess of state expenditure over state tax and earned income would raise demand and prices directly. The higher prices would choke back or 'crowd out' private demand, making room for the state's excess purchases. But, as we shall see, such a price rise would be self-terminating at a new, higher, price level. Continuously rising prices need a continuously rising money supply that continuously exceeds the contemporaneous demand for it. The economist's idea of 'demand for **money balances**' is a demand for money to *hold*, not (as the non-economist might think) for money to *spend*. If we regard transactions involving money as instantaneous, then all the money (i.e. coin, notes, chequable deposits) that the central bank has issued is in the possession of some individual, firm or institution. They hold it not because it is pretty but because a certain level of money balances – in the pocket, in the bank – gives the holder benefits, chiefly in terms of the convenience of *liquidity* – the ability to spend without forethought. Thus a stock of ready money is an *asset*. However, the convenience afforded by this asset must be balanced against the loss of income or pleasure due to holding one's wealth in this form. This 'opportunity cost' of holding money balances will be discussed again below; here it suffices simply to make the point that because there is an 'opportunity cost' to holding money, people will not hold unlimited amounts of it. And so, as the State, by writing cheques on its Reichsbank account, increased the supply of money balances in the bank accounts of individuals and firms, the recipients would find themselves in possession of more money than they wished to hold; and so would spend the excess, at least partly, on real assets such as stocks of materials or furnishings. And the price level would tend to rise.

But the increase in the money supply has to be continuous for the reason that, as prices rise, the money balances considered adequate to serve the needs of convenience, will also rise. Thus, a 'one-shot' rise in the money supply will only cause a self-terminating rise in prices. Eventually the rise in prices will have the result that firms and individuals consider that the higher level of money balances passing from buyer to seller round the economy is no longer excess to requirements. At this point the attempt to reduce money balances by extra spending will stop, and so prices will stop rising. Thus, for persistent inflation, fresh money balances must continually be being created by the Reichsbank's continuing financing of the budget deficit.

This also explains why the direct effect of a budget deficit in increasing aggregate demand is a less potent cause of inflation than the indirect effect of financing it by continuous monetary creation. In a full employment economy, excess government spending, financed, say, by borrowing from the private sector, will certainly raise prices. But the price rise will tend to leave firms and individuals short of desired money balances and they will try to remedy this shortage either by borrowing or by spending less. Borrowing cannot increase the total money supply, as *ex hypothesi*, this is unchanged; so it can only raise interest rates. (Interest rates will rise to the point where the incentive created for switching wealth from 'barren' money into interest-bearing assets makes people want to economise on the money balances they hold even at the higher prices, thus reconciling them to the unchanged money supply actually available.) Thus, budget deficits without monetary expansion will produce self-terminating price rises plus higher interest rates.

This is not an economics textbook and the above is a quite incomplete analysis. But I hope it conveys a sense of why economists say that changes in the supply of (or, as we shall see, the demand for) money were the engine of the monetary process of inflation (Webb, 1989, pp. 24f).

To the extent that the extra spending was satisfied by importing extra goods, the price-raising effect of spending excess money balances would be dampened. If foreigners had been willing to finance the resultant trade deficit, excess money balances would have caused little inflation in Germany – only a huge trade deficit. To the extent that they were unwilling, the attempt to buy the foreign currencies to pay for the excess of imports over exports would force the depreciation of the domestic currency against foreign. This is how the quantity theory connects the rising money supply to the depreciation of the mark.

As said above, quantity theory reasoning of the kind just expounded is integral to all theories of the inflation studied here. The hallmark of the quantity theory, as distinct from other theories, is that it regards the money supply as 'causing' the price level. From this it is a short step to regarding German fiscal and interest-rate policy as the autonomous causes of the inflation, causes which were under the control of the political authorities. This made the 'quantity theory' the favourite theory of the Allied (especially the French) politicians pressing for reparations payment, because it could underpin their claim that the German political authorities were contriving 'bankruptcy' (in the sense defined in chapter 2). Its reasoning seemed to imply that stabilising prices was a simple matter of closing the budget deficit and raising interest rates. The quantity theory did have distinguished but minority support inside Germany too (Ellis, 1934, pp. 215–36).

However, as an economic theory of the German inflation, the quantity theory suffers from two sorts of inconsistency with the evidence. Perused today, much of Bresciani-Turroni's classic work reads like a laboured defence of the quantity theory in the light of its awkward fit with the evidence.

Firstly, there was a tendency, at critical turning-points between the 'phases', for the exchange rate to change first, and for wholesale prices to follow its lead (Bresciani-Turroni, 1937, pp. 28–35). If inflation happened because increased government deficits raised domestic prices as outlined above, wholesale price changes should uniformly have preceded exchange-rate movements. This enabled contemporary 'balance of payments' theorists to challenge the claim regarding the autonomy of domestic fiscal and interest-rate policy, as the next section will explain.

Secondly, prices did not rise in step with the money supply as the quantity theory implies. This can be immediately shown from Figure 3.1 (p. 37), where the use of the logarithmic scale on the vertical axis enables us to interpret the slopes of the lines as rates of growth. Thus it shows clearly that whereas the rate of growth of the monetary base was fairly steady from 1916 to mid-1922, the rate of price rise was anything but steady. In particular, the money supply continued to grow, albeit more slowly, in 1920–1, while prices were falling. Further discussion of this problem is deferred to the next section but one.

### The balance-of-payments theory of the German inflation

'Balance-of-payments' theorists of the German inflation argued for a reverse causal sequence: exchange rate depreciation caused rising domestic prices, and these caused the budget deficit and the rise in the money supply. Although monetary expansion was necessary to the mechanism, it was not the exogenous, originating cause. The exchange-rate depreciation is the exogenous prime mover of this theory.

The exchange rate depreciated, so it was held, because the losses of territory, foreign investments and merchant shipping under the Versailles Treaty, plus reparations transfers, destabilised the German balance of payments (cf. pp. 11ff), thus creating an ineradicable excess of the demand for foreign exchange to buy imports and pay reparations, over the reduced supply of foreign exchange due to loss of invisible income. This excess demand made the mark depreciate against foreign currencies, and depreciation raised import prices in marks, with repercussions on all prices (Ellis, 1937, pp. 237–56).

However, most economists would say that, without monetary expansion, the rising prices would have tended to raise the demand for money in the same way as for a budget deficit, but that with an unchanged money supply interest rates would have risen and encouraged sufficient economising in the demand for money to reconcile it to the unchanged supply. The exchange rate would have fallen to make import prices sufficiently higher relative to home prices and incomes to reduce import spending enough to stabilise the **trade balance**. A new stable price level would have emerged – higher in domestic terms, lower in foreign currency terms, than the original, and with import prices higher relative to home prices than before. 'Balance-of-payments' theorists argued, however, that this new equilibrium was never reached, because of the effect of rising prices on the budget. German public expenditures, they said, were also rather irreducible in real terms, whilst the real value of tax receipts was eroded in times of rising prices by the inevitable lag of tax payment behind assessment (Moulton and McGuire, 1923, pp. 157ff). This made budgetary balance impossible without so reducing expenditure, or raising tax rates, as to throw Germany into economic chaos (Helfferich, 1927, p. 601). Raising interest rates would have the same effect. The Reichsbank had no realistic option except to finance the deficit by monetary expansion. German budget deficits and low interest rates were not freely reversible by the German authorities as the quantity theorists claimed: German economic survival depended on them. As the rising money supply raised German prices, so the trade balance deteriorated further, the mark fell further against foreign currencies, the cost of public expenditure rose, in an endless, vicious circle.

Thus the 'balance of payments' theory is a corollary of the 'structural' theory of the impossibility of making reparations transfers (p. 26), with another 'structural' imbalance added to it – that necessitating the budget deficit and low interest rates. Naturally, this theory had a strong following in Germany because it threw the main blame for inflation on the Versailles Treaty but it also attracted significant academic support in the USA (Williams, 1921–2; Angell, 1926, pp. 193–9; Ellis, 1937, pp. 237–56).

The 'balance of payments' theory as just expounded is incomplete, because it does not explain the financing of the 'structural' trade deficit. This depended on speculation in the mark (see p. 30). The mark always fell to a point which would stimulate sufficient speculation to finance reparations transfers plus the 'required' import surplus. Recognising these points, Graham argued that in 1919 a mix of budgetary causes and (from mid-year) intense import demand unrelieved by speculative counterdemand were the cause. These sources of inflation would have disappeared in 1921 but for the commencement of cash reparations transfers, which were decreasingly counterbalanced by speculation (Graham, 1930, pp. 76–7, 127–49, 172–3).

### Money demand and supply: 'expectational' theories of the inflation

As stated above, the major analytical shortcoming of the 'quantity theory' was, how to square an erratic rate of price increase with a rather steady (to 1922) rate of monetary expansion. If, as it supposed, demand for money balances kept pace with prices, prices would rise if, and only if, the money supply kept increasing.

But it has been fairly conclusively shown that the demand for money balances did not keep pace with prices. To show this, a means must be found of quantifying 'the demand for money balances'. If, following the practice of economists, we assume that nobody ever hangs on to unwanted money balances, or ever does without wanted balances, then, since the recorded stock of money must all be held by some persons, firms or public authorities, the stock of money held in the economy is always the stock people want to hold at that time. And therefore the statistics of the stock (or *supply*) of money held also always reveal the amount of money *demanded* at that moment. Did the stock of nominal money balances, then, simply rise so as to keep pace with rising prices? As already stated, we can track the development only of 'the monetary base' in this period, not the entire money supply. The bottom part of Figure 3.1 (p. 37) shows how the deflated, or real value of the base-money stock changed, relative to 1913. It shows that demand for money balances *relative to prices* changed all the time. From mid-1916 to mid-1920 the private sector and foreign investors' demand for mark money balances rose faster than prices (demand for real money balances became larger than before the war), despite the lower real national income. However, from 1919 their demand for money balances rose more slowly than prices (with a temporary reversal in 1920–1); i.e. demand for real money balances fell.

Contemporaries noticed this too, and mostly explained it by arguing that the normal tendency for the demand for money balances to keep pace with prices was interrupted by 'panic' or 'speculative' flights from the currency related to reparations crises (Graham, 1930, pp. 99–114; Bresciani-Turroni 1937, pp. 53–7, 60–3, 100–3, 150–74). But few succeeded in giving a rational account of 'panic' or 'speculation'. This really began when the monetarist revolution of the 1950s developed the 'opportunity cost' theory of demand for money. We have already seen the 'opportunity cost' of holding wealth as money balances in terms of the interest income foregone. There is also an 'opportunity cost' in holding wealth as money and not as goods if prices are expected to rise, and, finally, in domestic and not in foreign currency if the domestic currency is expected to depreciate. One can therefore hypothesise that, if domestic price inflation and/or nominal interest rates, and/or currency depreciation are expected to increase, the 'opportunity cost' of holding real money balances will be perceived to rise, and individuals and firms will economise on these balances. But note the following contrast: an *actual* price rise will *increase* the demand for money balances (so as to enjoy unchanged advantages of convenience from holding them), whereas an *expected* rise in prices will cause the demand for balances to rise less than actual prices (to reduce the expected loss of wealth as rising prices erode their value).

Cagan (1956) applied this theory to seven 'hyperinflations'. He hypothesised that the demand for real money balances (in the

German case, papermark circulation deflated by prices) would fall as the expected increase of prices rose, and vice versa. He had no direct evidence of price expectations. So he postulated that as recent actual past price changes accelerated or decelerated, expectations of future price changes accelerated or decelerated 'adaptively' according to a specific formula. He believed that he found statistically strong evidence of a stable inverse relationship between changes in the real demand for money balances and changing expected inflation, as inferred by this formula.

This implies that a change in the expectation of inflation can cause actual inflation without any change in the money supply. If expected inflation rises, the demand for money balances will fall, and people will spend the excess money balances, thus raising prices. In practice, as long as no other currency can be used for transactions, a limit is placed on the compressibility of real demand for the holding of money balances by the finite period that must elapse between acquiring and spending money.[3] Thus, in the long run, inflation cannot persist if the money supply does not expand. However changes in expected prices can also cause the money supply to expand in the following way. As already shown, a single 'one-shot' rise in expected inflation can cause inflation. If this has the effect of causing a budget deficit, as the 'balance of payments' theorists supposed, and the deficit is financed by increasing the money supply, which further raises prices, a single initiating change in expected inflation could engender an ongoing actual inflation.

Direct evidence about price expectations exists from 1921 in the form of quotations for the **forward exchange rate of the mark** (Einzig, 1937, pp. 21ff, 450ff). Frenkel (1979, 1982) used it to demonstrate a stable, negative relation between expected inflation and real demand for money. He also thought that expected inflation

---

[3] Graham (1930) argued that this physical limit to the fall in real balances demanded was reached in the last quarter of 1922, after which money could change hands no faster. In fact there was, paradoxically, an extreme shortage of cash in Germany at the end of the inflation, whilst the (nominal) supply of it was rising exponentially. When the price level rises forty-fold, as it did in September 1923, the entire note issue has to be replaced or overprinted several times a month. This could not be done fast enough (Webb, 1989, pp. 81–2; Rowley, 1994, pp. 115ff, 156ff). In this final period inflation was probably driven by the money-supply process described on pp. 48ff, rather than by falling real demand for money.

drove actual inflation by causing the money supply to expand, as just outlined.

But how are expectations formed? The development of thought on this matter is a large part of the history of macroeconomics in the 1970s and 1980s. Cagan's mechanical relation between recent and expected inflation was soon shown to be rather at odds with his 'quantity theory' presuppositions. Suppose that the quantity theory is true, and that for a long time the money supply and prices had risen at 3 per cent per annum but that the authorities now suddenly doubled the money supply. Prices would, more or less, double. But the expectation of inflation formed on Cagan's model would continue to run at 3 per cent. Market agents who formed their expectations 'adaptively' on Cagan's model would find themselves outsmarted by those who recognised the relation between price rises and the money supply. This example suggests that people will base 'rational' expectations of how much prices will rise on their notion of why prices rise.

Holtfrerich (1986) connected expectational changes to reparations crises. He inferred expectational changes from both changes in the 'forward' exchange rate and major inflexions in the level of real money balances, but noted that the two were not coincident. The fall in real balances sharply accelerated from the time of the 'London Ultimatum' of May 1921, but the forward exchange rate did not fall below the spot rate until July 1922. On the grounds that foreign exchange controls impeded German participation in international currency markets, he argued that the forward rate reflected foreign rather than German expectations about the mark. He therefore deduced that until July 1922 foreign pessimism about future inflation lagged behind domestic, but thereafter foreigners also joined in 'the flight from the mark' (but see also Frenkel 1982, pp. 184–93). However, he did not exactly argue that changes in expectations dragged along monetary expansion in their wake. Rather he explained monetary expansion, and hence inflation in the long run, as the result of the political choice of the German authorities in these years for budget deficits, low interest rates and high employment. Changing demand for money explained the short-run variability of inflation (Holtfrerich, 1983, 1986, pp. 66–72, 155–88, 192).

Steven B. Webb (1986, 1989) advanced the most thoroughgoing argument that inflationary expectations increased the money supply and drove the inflationary process. He rejected the 'balance of payments' theorists' view, however, that this happened as rising inflation widened the budget deficit. Following Bresciani-Turroni (1937, pp. 54–6), he notes that a faster rate of inflation tended to erode the real value of State expenditure more than of tax revenues (except in early 1919 and later 1923) thus narrowing rather than widening the real budget deficit (Webb, 1989, pp. 31–43). His theory focused on the split between 'market' and Reichsbank lending to the government to finance the continuing budget deficit. Until later 1921 the proportion of the treasury bill stock held outside the Reichsbank never fell below 50 per cent (Holtfrerich, 1986, pp. 67ff). Webb argued that firms and individuals bought bills when they expected that their real value at time of redemption would exceed the discounted purchase price sufficiently to offer an acceptable rate of return. As the repayment price was fixed in nominal terms, rising prices would reduce the real return – possibly making it negative. Webb envisaged potential bill-holders as approximately comparing the real value of the sum of all future expected **budget surpluses**[4] with the real value of the state's current outstanding debt. When the former exceeded the latter, the market would have the confidence that the debt could be repaid in money worth the same as that lent, and be likely to invest in the debt. When the latter exceeded the former, the market would doubt that the outstanding debt could be redeemed at a value that assured the holder of a profit in real terms, and would stop buying treasury bills. Because expectations are uncertain, and diverse, as long as some investors thought there was some chance of the debt being redeemed in money of the same value as that lent, 'the market' would continue to hold some of the treasury bill stock. But as fewer believed this, the proportion held by the Reichsbank as residual purchaser would have to rise; and therefore the rate of growth of the money stock would accelerate. Not only this: as expectations regarding future budget surpluses deteriorated, more of the large stock of existing (as opposed to new) treasury bills held by the market would be sold for

---

[4] Strictly speaking, the 'present value' of that sum.

cash. The Reichsbank would have to buy it to stop the **discount rate** on it from rising. This could cause the rate of growth of the current money supply to rise by more than that needed to finance the current actual deficit.

Given that the markets believed that the Reichsbank would always act as residual purchaser of treasury bills, when they calculated that future budget surpluses were insufficient to repay the current public debt, they would expect future inflation. This, then, would also reduce their real demand for money. The interaction between rising **monetisation** of State debt and falling real demand for money generates the inflation in Webb's theory.

Webb argued that expected future reparations payments dominated expectations of future budgetary balance. He supports this by co-relating evidence of (i) changing proportions of the treasury bill stock held by the market, (ii) changing demand for real money balances, and (iii) the mark forward exchange rate, with the timing of fiscal 'news' (only unexpected events in the fiscal sphere would alter the expectation of future budgetary balance). Thus he argued that in the second half of 1919 the unexpectedly severe Treaty terms made the market's expectations of future government expenditure rise by more than it expected Erzberger's new taxes to increase future revenues, so that hopes that future budget surpluses would suffice to redeem the current outstanding debt in real terms plummeted. However, by March 1920 the intervening price rise had reduced the real value of the government's domestic debt (mainly war debt) to about one-quarter of what it had been in May 1919. Hence market expectations of future surpluses rose and with them demand both for treasury bills and money balances revived, temporarily eliminating inflation. This optimism was shattered by the London Ultimatum, and both the market's holdings of the treasury bill stock and its real demand for money fell (Webb, 1989, pp. 49, 52).

From the end of 1922, Webb invoked a different inflationary mechanism. A doubling of the money supply when its real value is, say, 6bn goldmarks will enable the state to appropriate far more real goods and services than when its real value shrinks to, say, 600m goldmarks. As the real demand for money shrank, the attempt to acquire an undiminishing real level of goods and services through a budget deficit forced an exponentially increasing money supply – and price level.

## Wage and 'structural' theories of the German inflation

This approach maps, so to speak, the arguments of the balance of payments school on to the labour-market.[5] Where the balance-of-payments school had postulated an ineradicable balance of payments disequilibrium, Laursen and Pedersen (1964), following Robinson (1938), postulated an ineradicable labour-market disequilibrium. They argued that the inflation was the outcome of an unstable dynamic interaction between money wage demands, mark speculation and reparations. As the German exchange rate dropped (Laursen and Pedersen write 'rose' here, because they have in mind the price of the dollar in terms of marks), German money wages fell in dollar terms. This called forth a speculative counterdemand for marks on the part of those who, noticing the low dollar-equivalent German wages, argued that the mark must rise in the future to bring German dollar-wages in line with foreign dollar-wages. But it also caused workers to seek money-wage increases. And underlying their money-wage demands was a target real wage jacked up by the revolutionary upheavals, to a level that, at constant prices, would have eliminated the employers' profits, given the reduced post-revolutionary labour productivity levels. If the State had not acted to sustain aggregate demand, and raise prices (thus reducing real wages below those bargained for) bankruptcies and unemployment would have resulted, which would have tempered the workers' real wage demands – but also would have provoked civil disturbance. So the State always acted to raise demand and prices and maintain profitability. As workers therefore kept chasing their unattainable target, speculators' notions of the mark's future exchange-rate equilibrium fell progressively (though irregularly, as the reparations conflict also modified their stances: Laursen and Pedersen, 1964, pp. 55–63). Tschirbs (1982) documented the collusion of miners

---

[5] Laursen and Pedersen's analysis does without a concept of the supply of or demand for money.

and mineowners on the Reich Coal Council in securing price increases to offset wage increases and traced their success primarily
to the accommodating attitude of the state in view of the acute coal
shortage. But the question here is whether the state used inflation
to counteract the unemployment which high coal prices could have
caused elsewhere in the economy. In the model recently presented
by Burdekin and Burkett (1992), rising wage claims raised the rate
of monetary growth by signalling faster expected inflation and hence
causing market demand for treasury bills to fall, implying that the
market inferred a political will to conciliate labour.

Maier (1975, pp. 356–8; 1978; 1984) propounded a 'corporatist'
view of the German inflation. Denying that reparations caused it, he
regarded the inflation as the outcome of a 'tacit collusion' between
labour and capital. Businesses passed on wage concessions as price
increases, and benefited overall from the reducing real value of their
own debt. Business and labour both benefited from reduced tax liabilities as inflation reduced the real value of public debt. Their
benefit was at the expense of the *rentier* – whose assets consisted
of government and private fixed-interest bonds. The defect of this
theory is that according to the portfolio theory of wealth-holding
the rational wealth-holder will hold all kinds of assets. In normal
bourgeois society profit-earning capitalists and *rentiers* do not form
distinct social groups. Only as the inflation progressed, and the
wealthiest had the better opportunities to escape from it by cir-
cumventing foreign-exchange controls to acquire foreign-currency
assets, would a distinct, residual *rentier* class emerge, composed of
those less affluent *rentiers* who could not escape.

In these theories, monetary growth occurs because the state acts
to prevent the unemployment-causing consequences of the efforts
of sellers on some market or other to raise prices. Kindleberger
(1984a) supported a family of 'structural theories of the German
inflation', where the driving force is political stalemate over incompatible income claims. One variant of these is 'quantity-theoretic' –
the conflict is fought out over budget expenditure and taxation.
The second variant resembles the Laursen and Pedersen and Maier
theories in that it has incompatible income claims provoking wage
and price rises, which the Reichsbank passively accommodates by
monetary expansion so as to prevent unemployment. The main difficulty with the first is that the real non-reparations budget deficit

was declining (irregularly) from the end of 1919 to 1922 (Webb, 1989, p. 37), chiefly as the real value of (war) debt servicing shrank due to rapid inflation, and as the Erzberger taxes began to 'bite'. The main question for the second is whether the undeniable industrial conflict of the inflation era was its cause or its consequence. It is hard to prove that the innate income claims of the several classes were unusually irreconcilable in this period. Wants are intrinsically infinite: the market is a mechanism for reconciling initially irreconcilable demands. It is just as likely that the high levels of labour conflict during the inflation were caused by uncertainties over future inflation, as that they were exogenous causes of it.

## Searching for political causes of the inflation

'Structural' theories of the inflation have been the implicit favourite of many political historians. Very often these have 'piggy-backed' on a quantity theory view, but where the contemporary quantity theory was employed to support the charge that politicians willingly 'chose' inflation, quantity theory historians used the theory to connect the monetary expansion to domestic class-related political conflict, with the budget as the battlefield. Thus for example Witt's (1983) argument that the bourgeoisie sabotaged an 'integrated, proto-keynesian, economic, social and financial policy' for coping with the postwar transition (see p. 8), was also a theory of the inflation. Maier (1978) and to some extent Feldman (1977, pp. 8f) used something closer to the 'wage' theory, regarding inflation as a policy for assuaging the employment effects of industrial conflict between increasingly monopolistic groupings of capital and labour. They regarded inflation of this sort as, in some degree, endemic to industrial societies and particularly acute in post-armistice Europe because of the acute class tensions to which it was subject. In Feldman's (1982, p. 195) view, the temporary stabilisation of 1920–1 failed because '[t]he Great Fear of 1920–21 ... was that Germany would succumb to the high unemployment levels of those who had taken the deflationary path'.

The advance of globalisation since the 1970s means that the politicisation of markets no longer seems as integral to modern capitalism as it did, and a more contingent view opens up of market power during the inflation. The 'Central Co-operating Partnership' (see p. 5) had no real existence after 1919; bodies such as the 'Iron Trades Federation' appear as ephemeral, government-sponsored responses to political protest about the distributional inequities of an inflation that had other causes. The great business conglomerates formed in this period, which to contemporaries embodied the final stage of monopoly capitalism, seem now more like makeshift defences against price unpredictability (Feldman, 1977, pp. 148–59, 164–87, 210–79; 1993, pp. 272–300). After early 1919, the locus of labour market struggle was the public rather than the private sector (Kunz, 1986: 283–348). A political theory of the inflation focusing on domestic socio-political conflict would predict an inflation rate whose major inflexions coincided with domestic budgetary and labour crises; but as indicated at the start of the chapter, these usually coincided with foreign-policy crises. Nevertheless, the argument that the state's anxiety to conciliate labour was a significant factor in its failure to stop the inflationary process (until 1923) has solid archival support.

Feldman (1993) argues that in the period before May 1921, '... the chief causes of the inflation were endogenous ... ' – i.e. located in domestic political conflict. Up to May 1919 he places a 'structural' and quantity theory emphasis on the budgetary consequences of the demobilisation strategy (see p. 9). After mid-1919, he adds to this the autonomous momentum of the wage movement started by demobilisation policy, as workers chased rising prices. As already indicated, this subverted the temporary stabilisation of 1920–1, and its end was signalled by an invigorated trade-union 'assault' on the employer position from February 1921. His explanation of the acceleration of the inflation from May 1921 incorporates expectational elements. The reparations demands both destabilised exchange-rate expectations and sapped the domestic will to find solutions to the stabilisation problem. The only genuine opportunity to break the destabilising cycle of expectations, and both reach accommodation with the Allies and seriously increase taxation, was lost with the failure to form a 'great coalition' embracing the SPD and the 'business-orientated' DVP in November 1922. This would have spared Germany the misery of 1923 (Feldman, 1993, pp. 105–31, 156–73, 213–50, 418, 490, 504f).

Only the 'expectational' theory of Webb makes reparations conflict the main engine of inflation. From a quantity theory perspective, the budgetary burden of current 'Treaty expenses' cannot explain why inflation raged in 1919 (when these burdens had scarcely come on stream) and ceased in 1920 (after they had). Trying to argue, with the 'balance-of-payments' theorists, that actual reparations transfers were a major destabiliser of the exchange rate is also unsatisfactory, as these were a burden on the balance of payments for only the fifteen months or so from May 1921 to August 1922, when Germany more or less observed the London Plan. The 'structural theories' assign no role to reparations. But by making the expected impact of future reparations payments on expected future budgetary balance the central engine of the inflationary process, Webb's theory gives the reparations conflict (rather than reparations actually paid) a dominant place in the inflationary process. It implies that without reparations domestic labour politics might well have precipitated an inflation, but a far milder one. However 'expectational theories' also leave politics less firmly in charge of the process. They postulate, as the slippery link between policies and inflation, that elusive information processor – the 'mind of the market', which determined the demand for state debt and money balances.

Webb's theory pinpoints as crucial the failure of the German government to enunciate a credible stabilisation strategy before autumn 1923 (contrast the time-limited British Gold Embargo Act of 1920: Balderston, 1995b). Drawing on chapter 2, one might hypothesise that a number of factors prevented the enunciation of any credible stabilisation strategy and generated a volatile process of expectations-formation by the financial markets, which eventually ended in hyperinflation. These included: (i) the unpredictability of the reparations conflict because of the basic irrationality of the Allies' position, (ii) the undesirability of enunciating such a strategy before the reparations bill was finalised in May 1921, and (iii) the impossible political pressures on the Reich government because of its role as the fiscal agent of the Allies, given (iv) the acute fiscal fissure between left and right in German politics.

### The economic effects of the inflation

The now voluminous literature on the effects of the inflation has been ably surveyed by Hubbard (1990) and Feldman (1993, pp. 513–627, 837–58), and will be only briefly discussed here under three headings. Firstly, the contemporanous effects on aggregate real income and employment. Secondly, the effects on the distribution of income and wealth. Thirdly, the effects on longer-run economic growth. Space prevents discussion of the effects on politics or moral culture (Childers, 1982; Hughes, 1988; Jones, 1989; Feldman, 1993, pp. 513ff, 854–8).

Most historians would agree that, even without inflation, postwar Germany's per capita real income would have been lower than in 1913 because of the wartime neglect and decay of the German capital stock, the effect of the revolution on productivity, and the effect of the reparations conflict on the terms of trade. Laursen and Pedersen (1964, p. 123), Holtfrerich (1986, pp. 297–300), Abelshauser (1978) and Braun (1990, pp. 37–41) concur, if for varying reasons, that Germany would have been worse off, overall, under stable prices between 1919 and 1922. The actual effects of the inflation on German aggregate real income and employment at the time can (in the best economic-history tradition) only be gauged once some non-inflationary counterfactual has been specified. This counterfactual must imagine the actual reparations regime and reparations payments made as unchanged, in order to isolate the 'sheer' effects of inflation.

On this presumption, the quantity theory implies that, since the 'Erzberger' revenues were coming on stream, with a little more effort in raising taxes/cutting domestic expenditure, price stability could have been perpetuated. But Germany would not have received speculative inflows of capital and the quantity theory provides no clear answer to the question of whether she could have borrowed successfully abroad. If not, her terms of trade with abroad might still have been worsened by the need, unrelieved by speculative inflows, to force exports on still-hostile foreign markets. The effect on domestic unemployment depends on how wages would have responded to stable prices. The consensus would probably be that workers would have achieved a higher real wage; and that higher unemployment would have ensued. However, with intelligent floating of the currency, Germany might still have escaped the worst of the postwar depression as France did. The supply-side effects on worker effort are unclear: maybe stable prices would have reduced conflict. As the absence of speculation in the mark is the most certain of these effects it seems that, on quantity theory presuppositions, Germany would have been worse off under stable prices after 1920 – at least if one excludes the nightmare of 1923 – unless the reparations regime had improved as a result.

Webb's 'expectational' theory implies that without the prospect of long-run agreed reparations reduction, permanent price stability could only have been achieved in 1920–1 if the markets had somehow come to believe in Germany's powers to resist Allied demands (an alliance with the USSR?). This would have made the chances of a reparations loan so much the less, the pressure on the terms of trade so much the greater. Thus, on the expectational theory, there would have been even less advantage from stabilisation in 1920 – again excluding 1923. The general presumption of the 'structural' theories is that a better solution to the internal distributional problem would have flowed from a rational domestic political settlement, than from the chaotic effects of the distributional conflicts. But they do not imply a counter-factually higher or lower real national income under stable prices, unless these had facilitated reparations revision.

However Ferguson (1996, 1998) argued that, with stabilisation in 1920 and no speculative support for the mark, the export pressure from Germany on Allied unemployment would have been more severe from 1921 and forced the Allies into earlier revision of reparations. In his (1995, pp. 273–84) view fairly easy political choices not to subsidise shipbuilding and public-sector employment could have secured stabilisation in 1920. But as on this argument price stabilisation had to precede revision of the London Plan, the expectational theory suggests more difficulty.

The redistributive effects of inflation are well described in English-language works (Hubbard, 1990; Holtfrerich, 1986, pp. 221ff). The main wealth redistribution was from creditors to debtors when inflation exceeded what was expected when the debt contract was concluded. The annihilation of internal war debt made the German taxpayer the greatest beneficiary. But as stated above, portfolio diversification should have limited many wealth-redistributional effects. It was the small *rentier* – the 'widows and orphans', the house-owners, whose wealth was least diversified, who probably suffered most. Real assets should have kept more of their value, but the lacklustre performance of the deflated share-price index shows that even these were affected by the uncertainty (Webb, 1989, p. 86; Bresciani-Turroni, 1937, pp. 253–85). However with deflation and a slump, share prices would have fallen more.

Real wages and salaries did tend to move inversely with the rate of inflation (Holtfrerich, 1986, pp. 233ff), and at the time the left believed that capitalists used inflation to exploit workers. Holtferich (1986, pp. 247f, 265ff) and Abelshauser (1978) claimed, however, that the real wage fell less than the average per capita real incomes of all Germans, but that employment was maintained because inflation raised investment demand. Scholz (1986) and Tschirbs (1986) have challenged this claim, but the nominal wage and price data, let alone the real national income calculations, are too shaky to support definite assertions. Employment was also sustained in this period by the swollen public-sector employment which budget deficits helped to sustain.

Inflation severely compressed pay differentials within both the salary-earning and wage-earning groups, and between them (Holt-frerich, 1986, pp. 231–48). But below the unskilled, in the stratum of the poor dependent on welfare payments, it seems probable that inflation caused catastrophic hardship by eroding the real value of benefits (Niehuss, 1986). It should also be noted that the low exchange rate redistributed real income from purchasers of imports to the producers of exports or of import-competitive goods, benefiting, for example farmers and the coal industry. On the other hand, State controls on rents, farm prices, retail markups – all acting on behalf of the urban consumer – and, eventually, the terms of the revaluations of debts in 1925 superimposed a further income and wealth redistribution. It was these political modifications of inflationary outcomes that generated the most protest (Moeller, 1982; Lyth, 1990).

The debate about the longer-run effect of the inflation on German economic growth focuses on real investment. The traditional consensus was that this was stimulated by inflation. There were extensive investment programmes in the Ruhr steel industry, in merchant shipping and in railway rolling stock (Graham, 1930, pp. 242–3; Bresciani-Turroni, 1937, pp. 199–202, 277–9; Miercejeweski, 1999, pp. 44–6). Earlier writers (e.g. Bresciani-Turroni, 1937, p. 390) argued that negative real interest rates stimulated an excess demand for capital goods that resulted in excess capacity in the capital goods sector after 1924. However, postwar Keynesian economic historians argued that this excess capacity simply resulted from the deflationary gold-standard policies after 1924 (Holtfrerich, 1986, pp. 204–6; Laursen and Pedersen, 1964, pp. 95–8). Abelshauser and Petzina (1981) built this into a more comprehensive argument. Following the Hungarian economist Janossy, they postulated that deterioration of the physical capital during the war forced the path of German aggregate output below a growth trend implicit in the reproduction of its **human capital** stock. This raised the yield on real investment, and high real investment would have propelled a temporarily faster rate of growth until the relationship between the physical and human capital stock normalised again – roughly at the point where per capita output regained the level it would have reached if the war had never occurred. The high investment of the inflation represented this temporarily faster growth, but it was curtailed by misguided monetary policies after 1924. Thus, in their view, Germany had a truncated reconstruction phase after the First World War, in contrast to the full reconstruction after 1945.

But Lindenlaub (1985) showed from research into the business histories of three large machine-building firms that their inflation-period investment in plant and equipment was in fact abnormally low, and that investment decisions tended to be postponed because of the acute price uncertainty (cf. Webb, 1989, pp. 85–9). In the light of this evidence the peculiarity of the steel and shipping industries and the railways became obvious: all of them had to spend State compensation for Treaty forfeitures. Lindenlaub's view of inflation-period investment agrees with the evidence of the mediocre real level of share prices. However Table 3.2 shows some supply-side estimates of real investment in Germany in the inflation. These suggest that investment in buildings (dominated by public sector investment) was low, but that investment in equipment and machinery, whilst lower than in 1913, was higher, in relation to the same kind of investment in the later 1920s, than was the case in the UK.

Other long-term effects include those on the German capital market (Balderston, 1985).

Table 3.2. Supply-side indicators of fixed investment in Germany 1913, 1920–9, with UK comparison

| Year | German fixed investment indicators | | | UK fixed investment | |
| | Real domestic consumption | | | | |
| | Real domestic purchases of machinery | Constructional steel | Cement | Plant and equipment | Non-residential buildings |
| --- | --- | --- | --- | --- | --- |
| 1920 | 101 | n.a. | 37 | 99 | 105 |
| 1921 | 101 | n.a. | 48 | 144 | 88 |
| 1922 | 112 | 66 | 75 | 113 | 83 |
| 1923 | 74 | 47 | 54 | 123 | 96 |
| 1924 | 85 | 61 | 63 | 130 | 101 |
| 1925 | 110 | 75 | 88 | 149 | 116 |
| 1926 | 84 | 73 | 87 | 139 | 100 |
| 1927 | 121 | 107 | 108 | 158 | 101 |
| 1928 | 136 | 78 | 115 | 177 | 100 |
| 1929 | 127 | 87 | 105 | 165 | 118 |
| **Averages** | | | | | |
| 1920–3 | 97 | 56 | 54 | 120 | 93 |
| 1924–9 | 110 | 80 | 94 | 153 | 106 |

*Note:* 1913 = 100.
*Source:* Balderston (1993), p. 74.

## The economics of stabilisation

Long before the end of 1923 Germans had abandoned the 'papermark' for pricing purposes. They used instead the abstraction of '**goldmark**' pricing (Rowley, 1994, pp. 75ff). Earlier still, Germans had abandoned the mark as a 'store of value'. Those who could acquired foreign-currency assets. Those who couldn't took flight into 'real values' – physical assets. But papermark notes (including 'emergency moneys') and papermark deposits remained the main means of retail payment. To make payment Germans turned 'goldmark' into 'papermark' prices at the current dollar exchange rate. On 15 November 1923 a new, temporary, internal currency, called the rentenmark, was officially introduced, initially with a floating exchange rate against the papermark. It was theoretically redeemable into bond liabilities secured on 'mortgages' imposed by decree on German real estate. The real-estate owners paid a new rentenmark tax as the 'interest' on this new so-called mortgage liability; and this paid the interest on the rentenmark bonds. On 20 November, the papermark's external value was successfully stabilised at 4.2 million million to the dollar, and its internal exchange rate to the rentenmark at 1 million million. Thus the rentenmark was made the embodiment of one 'goldmark', as, though not officially convertible into dollars, it was implicitly stabilised at the prewar par of 4.2 to the dollar.

Already in August the Reichsbank had stated that it would stop financing budget deficits by the end of 1923, and in fact ceased to do so from November. The Rentenbank – the new institution issuing rentenmarks – extended a single credit to the government to carry it over until its newly index-linked tax revenues began to flow in sufficiently. Meanwhile, using special enabling legislation, the government acted to balance its budget by dismissing about one quarter of its employees, reforming unemployment relief, and by changing the assessment rules and accelerating the due payment dates for its revenues. Emergency decrees relaxed the stringency of the eight-hour day to meet business fears over its competitiveness, strengthened the wage-arbitration machinery as a way of defending collective labour contracts against employer attack and on behalf of the penniless unions, and imposed an utterly niggardly revaluation of state debt – though this had to be modified in June 1925 (Holtfrerich, 1986, pp. 301–30; Feldman, 1993, pp. 807–9).

Because the exchange rate of the papermark began to slip again in early 1924, on 7 April the Reichsbank imposed a ceiling limiting its future **discounting** to the rate at which its present bill stock reached **maturity** (Hardach, 1976, pp. 35–40). This 'Kreditstopp' halted economic recovery from the crisis of 1923 and unemployment and bankruptcies shot up over the summer of 1924. Finally, a new international gold standard currency, the 'reichsmark', was introduced in September 1924, and the Dawes Plan placed the Reichsbank under the supervision of a Control Council, half of whose members were foreign, and severely limited its lending to the Reich (Northrop, 1938). Along with restoration of the gold standard went commitment to participation in a liberal international trading system.

Quantity theorists would attribute the success of this stabilisation solely to the political will to restrict the money supply and stop the budget deficit. On the 'balance of payments' theory, the actual suspension of reparations payments had been the vital precondition for this. On the 'wage' and 'structural' theories, all sides realised that waging distributional conflict via budget deficits and inflation no longer yielded results. On the 'expectational theory', the downward revision of inflation expectations caused a large rise in the demand for money which halted inflation and increased the real value of tax receipts – so that budgetary balance was a consequence rather than cause of stabilisation (Franco, 1990). But the 'expectational theory' has a harder job explaining the downward revision of inflation expectations, as (*contra*: Sargent, 1982; Webb, 1989, p. 62). Poincaré had not agreed to substantial reparations reductions in October 1923 when he agreed to the establishment of the Dawes Committee. Probably the pain of the unemployment and bankruptcies that followed the 'Kreditstopp' of April 1924 were needed to convince the markets that Germany was committed to a 'gold standard' regime (Dornbusch, 1987; modifying Sargent, 1982).

The persistent trade deficit of the following years has been treated as evidence that, like the UK, Germany restored the gold standard at an overvalued rate, necessitating a deflationary monetary policy (Braun, 1990, p. 59). However this view attributes to policy a 'degree of freedom' it didn't possess. By the autumn of 1923 prices in Germany were generally fixed in 'goldmark' terms. As we have seen, 'goldmark' prices converted seamlessly into rentenmark prices. But had the authorities chosen to fix the rentenmark at, say, 8/42 of a dollar, then rentenmark prices would simply have been 25 per cent higher, so as to express goldmark prices, and the relation between German and world prices would have been unaffected by their choice. The German real exchange rate was *low* in 1924 and the import surplus has another explanation (see chapter 4).

# 4
# Normalisation and stagnation?
# 1924–1929

The years 1924–9 have often been described as the 'golden years' of the Weimar Republic. 'Gold-plated' might be more apt. Prices stabilised as Germany restored the gold standard. The Franco-German Trade Agreement of 1927, following the Treaty of Locarno (1925) seemed to signal the return of harmonious international economic relations. Output revived, except in the sharp, rather enigmatic, but mercifully short slump of 1925–6. Exports bounced back from 1924 levels; however, imports rose even faster (except in 1926), financed by heavy foreign borrowing, which supported rising private and public consumption. A succession of weak centre-right cabinets, without the SPD but sometimes including the DNVP and all dominated by Stresemann, governed between the two Reichstag elections of 1924 and 1928. The rise of the SPD vote in the election of June 1928 plus the growing intransigence of the DNVP produced a precarious 'Great Coalition' of SPD, Centre Party, DDP and DVP that broke up because of growing resistance on the right to the tax regime that supported Weimar's 'welfare capitalism'. It was replaced by Brüning's minority cabinet. Major social policy developments included tax-subsidised housing finance from 1924 (Witt, 1979), unemployment insurance in 1927 (Führer, 1990) and evolving municipal welfare programmes. Real wages rose significantly, though only broadly regaining their 1913 level by 1927. The labour-market compromises of 1918 remained fiercely contested. The concessions made to business in autumn 1923 over the eight-hour day were rescinded by the State in 1927–8 and the labour arbitration decrees of the same era (see p. 59), which were resented by business, culminated in the Ruhr steel lockout of November 1928, with its unclear resolution.

The chapter will start by discussing the gold standard.

## Monetary policy and the gold standard

As the new President of the Reichsbank (from December 1923), Hjalmar Schacht kept the Bank's discount rate on the high side to solidify the credibility of the restored German gold standard. In summer 1924 it was still 10 per cent. From autumn 1924, however, it was undercut by the rates that foreign, especially US, money markets charged on short-term loans and discounts to Germany, and as a result borrowers ceased discounting bills at the Reichsbank. The discount restrictions imposed by the Reichsbank in April 1924 (see p. 59) were therefore terminated in December 1925.

Between 1924 and 1928 – more strictly, in 1924, most of 1925 and in 1927–8 – Germany accumulated a foreign debt thought to equal about 25 per cent of national income. (Some of this gross foreign debt was offset by German 'capital flight' to abroad.) Government authorities (mainly municipal), credit institutions (mainly mortgage banks) and private and public enterprises floated foreign bonds. Municipal access to foreign bond markets was controlled from the end of 1924 by the Advisory Council on Foreign Credits (McNeil, 1986, pp. 35–68, 180ff, 199ff), so they were also large domestic bond issuers. But interest rates on long-term domestic debt were even higher than on short-term, perhaps because of residual inflation uncertainty in Germany (Balderston, 1993, pp. 184–203), and 'blue chip' business corporations had found New York dollar loan offer terms superior to those needed for successful domestic bond flotation. Of private-sector (nonbank) bond issues, 70 per cent were made abroad in this period. The statistics on German foreign short-term borrowing are poor, but it has been estimated at twice the scale of German long-term foreign borrowing. US banks offered short credits to German borrowers, including local authorities, thus placing the German banks under competitive pressure, which they partly met by accepting foreign-currency deposits and re-lending these as foreign-currency loans to their customers. By mid-1928, 40 per cent of all deposits at the German 'great' banks were foreign deposits.

It was argued on page 30 that the consistent net foreign borrowing may have suggested private-sector optimism about future income growth. Another sign of optimism was the willingness of the banks to allow the value of their borrowed capital to rise more rapidly than that of their total assets, reducing the ratio of their own capital to borrowed capital. They did this to 'stay in the game' in an era of intense competitive pressure from other domestic as well as from US banks (Balderston, 1991). But it meant that if their total assets lost value (due, say, to loan defaults) they would soon become **insolvent** – and this happened in 1931.

This German collective tendency to borrow in excess of saving had to be matched by a willingness of foreigners to lend. Their willingness increased until early 1927, as registered by the decline in the excess of German over US short rates of interest (Figure 4.1). One reason for this could well have been the success of Schacht's credibility policy. The gold and foreign exchange reserves of the Reichsbank rarely dipped below 70 per cent of the value of the reichsmark note issue between 1924 and 1929 – well above the statutory minimum cover of 40 per cent. Keynesian economic historians criticised Schacht for feeding his gold-standard addiction with a

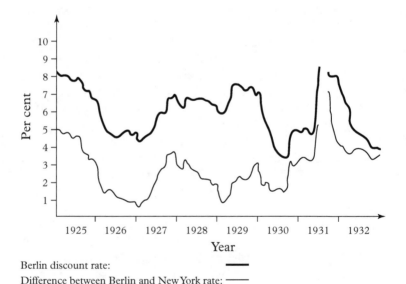

Berlin discount rate:                                        ▬▬▬
Difference between Berlin and New York rate: ─────

Figure 4.1 Berlin market discount rates and differential against New York rate, 1925–32, from Balderston, 1993, pp. 142, 147. Note: The break in the graph in 1931 is due to the impossibility of representing the high German interest rates of July–August on the scale used.

deflationary policy that depressed aggregate demand, employment, and capital-stock utilisation, and thus suppressed investment (Hardach, 1970; Petzina, 1977, pp. 95f). Stated this baldly (its authors in fact hedged it with qualifications), this view exaggerates Schacht's room for manoeuvre. In a globally integrated capital market, one (small) country's central bank cannot both opt for fixed exchange rates and for control of the domestic interest rate. It is stuck with the 'world' interest rate, plus whatever 'risk premium' the global financial markets charge on loans to the country in question. If it tries to reduce this interest rate, it will be forced to let its currency depreciate. If it tries to increase it, its interest rate will become irrelevant; borrowers will simply borrow abroad (as described above). And if it floats its currency, domestic-currency annualised interest rates can be reduced only by the percentage below the world rate that the global markets expect the currency to appreciate in the near future. Only if it imposes currency and capital controls, can it sovereignly control both domestic interest rates and exchange rates. Thus, to the extent that Schacht convinced the US money markets than the reichsmark–dollar exchange rate was inviolable, German interest rates would tend to converge towards US interest rates plus some irreducible risk premium.

By early 1927 German short rates had fallen to only $1/2$ per cent above US rates (Figure 4.1). Schacht's restrictive policies seem to have convinced the US markets that they could discern a German **policy regime** that would make defence of the reichsmark–dollar rate its overriding priority. This involved monetary policy as just described, and a fiscal policy that did not challenge this monetary policy by an improvidence that might, in the future, make politicians seek to finance state debt at interest rates which forced monetary expansion (see p. 38). The tone of the twice-yearly Reports of the Agent General for Reparations served until summer 1927 as a certification of German fiscal prudence. It is likely, then, that in this period the Reichsbank's gold-standard policy reduced interest rates, rather than raising them. (Whether US monetary policy imparted a deflationary bias to the world economy in this period is a different question.)

Ritschl (1998, p. 53) argues that the Dawes Plan, and particularly its 'transfer protection clause', acted as a further incentive to foreign lending. This was because, if the future repayment of foreign debt tended to weaken the exchange rate, the clause would require the Agent-General to suspend reparations transfers into foreign currencies. As a result, extra lending to Germany would have no net effect on the future stability of the reichsmark. The transfer clause would not of itself reduce the tax burden on debtors, for even during transfer suspensions reparations would still be collected out of taxation and transferred to the Reichsmark account of the Agent-General. It can be argued that the low debt-levels left by the 1925 revaluation laws, plus the fact that the Reich had taken responsibility for raising most of the taxes on which the municipalities (*via* tax transfers) were dependent, encouraged borrowing, but maybe municipal borrowing was not in fact unduly high in this era (Balderston, 1993, pp. 237–8).

From March 1927 German short-term interest rates drifted upwards of US short rates again. (The dip in early 1929 (see Figure 4.1, p. 63) reflects an unsustainably low Reichsbank rate: Balderston, 1993, pp. 157f.) But as the explanation of this belongs to the story of the German slump, I shall defer it until Chapter 5.

### Growth performance in the era of stabilisation

Before the 1960s, the general view was that German economic growth picked up after the stabilisation of the mark. This ushered in an era in which 'rationalisation' became the driving notion in business-management circles. Vague and elusive in its meaning, its core idea had to do with organisation: of industries, of firms, of working practices within firms, and hence of labour relations. Early accounts used the idea of 'rationalisation' to paint the picture of a massive, concerted and effective 'economic recovery' by German industry (Meakin 1928; Angell, 1929; Warriner, 1931; Brady, 1933). This impression was deepened by a spate of high-profile, mammoth amalgamations. Four in particular dominated the headlines.

Firstly, the formation of I.G. Farben as a unitary firm in 1925 out of looser prewar and wartime alliances of chemical firms involved in synthetic dyestuffs manufacture – hence the name: *Farben* (Hayes, 1987, pp. 11–16). This was effectively a monopoly trust of the most research-intensive German chemical firms (Plumpe, 1990, pp. 176–82). The aim of I.G. Farben was to create an effective unit for competing in the world arena, because the forfeiture of German chemical patent rights under the Versailles Treaty had destroyed the previous basis of Germany's domination of global dyestuffs and artificial fertiliser markets.

The second great amalgamation was the steel combine, Vereinigte Stahlwerke, in 1926 (Feldenkirchen, 1987). This new combine, including elements from the wartime and inflation-period Stinnes concern (this had crashed in 1925), was formed essentially to solve the short-term debt problems of its founder firms, but it ruthlesssly closed down older plant and concentrated output to exploit economies of scale. Whilst it dominated the steel and coal industries and was a large player in the engineering industries due to the vertical integration of its constituent firms, its policies could not ignore the challenge of other great steel firms, such as Krupps, Gutehoffnungshütte/M.A.N. and Klöckner.

Thirdly, the amalgamation of Daimler and Benz in 1926 was of a smaller scale in terms of capital involved, output and employment, but involved two of the most viable firms in the emergent car industry (Feldman, 1995, pp. 214ff; Gregor, 1998, pp. 20ff).

Fourthly, the amalgamation of two of Germany's largest banks, the Deutsche Bank and the Diskonto-Gesellschaft, in 1929, was designed to reduce costs and, possibly, to meet the competition of US banks on the German credit market (Feldman, 1995, pp. 230ff).

Amalgamation projects did not always succeed. The amalgamation of Daimler and Benz coincided with the failure to negotiate a larger 'auto trust', and talks about amalgamating the two electrical giants, Siemens and AEG, foundered on the opposition of C. F. von Siemens (Feldenkirchen, 1999, pp. 274–6). However, the social and business sciences of the day believed unanimously that concentration was essential to economic growth. Academic and journalistic commentators would have been astonished to learn of the importance now attached to the role of medium-sized industrial firms in (West) Germany's postwar growth. To them, smaller and medium-sized firms were doomed to extinction. Whether socialist or bourgeois, business leaders or trade unionists, and whether with approval or regret, Weimar contemporaries had no doubt that productivity advances went with a rising scale of production, and this required giant firms. Thus, when they saw these firms cutting out the dead wood of their inheritances, closing inefficient plants, and streamlining the product mix of the plants they retained in order to maximise economies of scale, they saw their conception of 'rationalisation' and its potential verified. They seized on evidence of implementation of American mass production methods.

Even without amalgamation, industry relations could be 'rationalised'. The autonomous but State-subsidised Reich Agency for Efficiency was established in 1921 to promote it, partly as industry's counter-move to the more State-led ideas about industrial efficiency through planning which Rathenau and Moellendorf had promoted during the war (see p. 4), and partly to empower business to rise to the challenge of exporting in the hostile postwar international environment. One of the main activities of this Agency was to facilitate the difficult negotiations for establishing interfirm 'norms' or standard sizes and fits to facilitate US-style interchangeability of parts.

Contemporary commentators credited cartels, too, with the power to bring order out of capitalist anarchy, to enable firms to survive recessions, and even to moderate the recessions themselves. Such effects would aid business calculation and hence business investment. Cartels had become moribund in the sellers' markets of the inflation, except for those enforced by the State. With the stabilisation, a denser network of cartels sprang up than had existed before the war; cartelisation encouraged counter-cartelisation (Nocken, 1974). However, relatively few of the 5,000 or so cartels often quoted as existing in Germany were 'strict' cartels – i.e. cartels limiting output by setting output quotas for member firms, and prescribing prices. For that degree of 'strictness', homogeneity of product, exclusion of outsider competitors (often by tariffs, though in cases like coal simply by high transport costs) and a relatively small number of producers (to enable policing against 'free-riding') were necessary. Strict cartels existed in coal, iron and steel, potash, artificial fertilisers, cement, bricks, papermaking and like industries. Most German cartels were 'condition cartels' principally regulating the terms of sale. Leading examples were the Association of German Machine-Builders and the Central Association of German Banks and Bankers. Such cartels were also common in the textile industries (Michels, 1928, pp. 170ff).

International cartelisation also increased in the later 1920s (Stocking and Watkins, 1948). The best-known example was the International Crude Steel Cartel of 1926–30, which was formed by German, French, Belgian and Luxembourg producers in order to cope with the postwar excess capacity resulting from Germany's replacement of the capacity lost in Lorraine. International cartelisation was particularly dense in the products of the electrical and chemical industries.

Optimistic accounts of economic growth in the 'golden twenties' came under challenge when the national income estimates of Hoffman *et al.* (1965) showed a lower **investment ratio** in the years 1925–9 (on average) than before 1913. This suggested, to the Keynesian theory of the day, that wrongheaded deflationary monetary policy in pursuit of a gold-standard fetish had depressed economic growth (cf. p. 57).

This account blamed the policymakers for slow post-stabilisation growth. It was challenged in 1978–9 by the Munich economic historian Knut Borchardt. He instead attributed the low investment ratio of that era to the pressure of wage demands. He argued that the real wage stood higher in 1929, relative to 1913, than did the real labour productivity of the economy as a whole, and that the reason for this was the system of compulsory wage arbitration that emerged in 1923–4, which dominated wage setting for the remainder of the Weimar Republic (James, 1986, pp. 209ff; Balderston 1993, pp. 30ff; Liu, 1999, pp. 110ff). A 'social agenda' had governed the wage norms that the arbitrators, influenced by the Reich Labour Ministry, were seeking to achieve and had ridden roughshod over economic realities. It had crippled the central engine of capitalist progress – investment – by squeezing profits through its wage settlements. To this was added the tax burden of the welfare transfers conducted by the various levels of the Weimar State, which raised the share of public expenditure from about 17 per cent of net national product (NNP) in 1913 to about 30 per cent in the later 1920s. Civil service salary hikes, especially in 1927, have been credited with exciting private-sector emulation (von Kruedener 1985; James, 1986, pp. 39ff, 218f; Clingan, 2001, pp. 138ff). Borchardt regarded this 'political economy' as necessary to the political stability of the republic. In his view, only robust growth could have softened the distributional antagonisms of the time but the effects of the wage and social policies on profits retarded investment and growth. Only a fundamental reform of the political economy of 'labourism' (cf. p. 8) could have restored the German economy to health. Borchardt (1991) believed that the shock of the slump did this by weakening the demands of labour. Unfortunately, by politicising wage determination as well as social policy, the Weimar Republic had alienated all protagonists in the fierce distributional conflict of the day so that the republic's social strategy for legitimising itself ended up by de-legitimising it.

Similarly, the optimistic view of Weimar business concentration was challenged by Harold James. Appealing to Olson (1982), he argued that amalgamation and cartelisation in this era revealed risk-aversion and entrepreneurial failure, and created a 'sclerotic', immobile economy. The much vaunted 'rationalisation' was in fact a public relations sham. German industry lost its dynamism so that, whereas the dispersion of industrial growth rates is wide in a dynamic economy when thrusting, new industries are pushing out effete old ones, it was rather narrow in the Weimar Republic. Reckendrees (2000, pp. 566ff) has recently illustrated this by arguing that Vereinigte Stahlwerke was overcapitalised, because the real aim of the amalgamation was to avert the potential bankruptcy of its founder firms (none the less, the firm dramatically raised productivity by closing obsolete plant). James (1986, pp. 110–61) blames the stagnancy on (i) the investment-inhibiting effects of high business taxation; (ii) the Republic's encouragement of corporatism: that is, of the replacement of market determination of prices and wages by politicised negotiations and cosy business agreements, thus weakening the incentive for enterprise; (iii) the cautious lending policies of the great banks favouring 'old' industries such as textiles, as investigations of the industrial distribution of bank lending at the end of the 1920s seemed to reveal; and (iv) the renascence of virulent agrarian protectionism from 1925 as tending to provoke money-wage demands.

In sum, a new view of the growth performance of the post-stabilisation years was created. It was not impressive, nor could it have been impressive merely with more sensible macroeconomic management. The economy was 'sick' and the political contradictions of the Republic had created an economic environment that made capitalism unviable. The Borchardt–James view was certainly consistent with the vehemence of business protest against the wage and taxation policies of the State, which culminated in the dramatically entitled pamphlet *Aufstieg oder Niedergang?* ('Recovery or Collapse?') issued by the 'peak' business association at the end of 1929. And it is consistent with the aims of heavy industry when it locked out one quarter million steel workers in November 1928, challenging an arbitrated wage award and precipitating the largest industrial dispute in the history of the Republic.

Albrecht Ritschl has dubbed this thesis 'Borchardt Thesis I' – to distinguish it from Borchardt's other thesis about fiscal policy in the slump, discussed in chapter 5. There are already good, if slightly dated, English surveys of the debate it provoked (Borchardt, 1990; Kershaw, 1990; von Kruedener, 1990).

There was, firstly, a debate about the wage and productivity statistics. Holtfrerich (1990b) soon showed various flaws in Borchardt's own calculations, some of which were partially rebutted by von Kruedener (1985). Ritschl (1990) rescued Borchardt's thesis by convincingly arguing that the standard NNP series (Hoffmann, 1965) exaggerated the output in the later 1920s relative to 1913 and substituting more plausible output estimates derived from the contemporary statistician Rolf Wagenführ. (The implication of this is, however, that the investment ratio was higher than the Hoffmann series had implied.)

Secondly, there has been a debate about whether the actual practices of the Arbitrators really did raise wages above some notional free-market rate. Archival studies have reached opposite conclusions on this point. Broadberry and Ritschl (1994) argued econometrically that the rising real wages tended to reduce the demand for labour in interwar Germany (cf. Corbett, 1994), but that this effect was overborne by the effect of **capital imports** in raising demand for goods and services and hence the derived demand for labour. The fact that the rise in employment was fastest in such **non-tradables** sectors, like building, supports their view against the earlier arguments of Balderston, who had attributed rising employment to rising exports. Balderston (1993, p. 40) also maintained that the higher real wages were necessary to raise the supply of labour: if the adult **participation rate** of 1928 had remained that of 1925, unemployment would have been minus 20,000! On the other hand, the demand for labour in the Weimar Republic was insufficient to stimulate immigration, unlike pre-1913 Germany and the post-1948 Federal Republic.

This leads, thirdly, to the debate about the effects of rising real wages on investment. Voth (1995) argued that there is a robust, positive statistical relationship between real wages and investment, but he did not specify the economic mechanism behind it. Broadberry and Ritschl (1994) argued that there was econometric evidence of the dependence of business investment on the realised level of business profits and hence an inverse relationship between investment and wages. The high cost of external finance in this period makes this plausible. The evidence that business profits really were low in this period has recently been strengthened by Spoerer's (1996) examination of a sample of the hitherto unexploited 'tax balance sheets' of the period, which were prepared to more stringent asset-valuation standards and not published. He could correlate these to other evidence to show that, unlike in the later 1930s, concealed profits were quite slight.

Finally, the striking German export performance in this period has been counterposed to Borchardt's pessimistic assessment of German competitiveness (Balderston, 1993, pp. 99ff; Tilly and Huck, 1994, pp. 53ff). But most economic historians now probably support a moderate version of the Borchardt–James thesis that wage growth exceeded productivity growth in the mid-Weimar years.

### The record of innovation

The discussion of the previous section rested on the highly abstract evidence of the statistics of aggregated output on the one hand, and of aggregate labour and capital inputs on the other. A more direct way of investigating the dynamism of the Weimar economy is to try to describe its innovative record (Dornseifer, 1995; Cantwell, 1995).

Recent economic analysis has distinguished global innovation from local innovation. Global innovation can be thought of as the advance of the world's technology frontier. Local innovation can be thought of in terms of the country or region in question 'catching up' on the global advance.

An impressionistic generalisation would be that before 1914 Germany exercised global leadership in organic chemical and pharmaceutical technology, and in some other fields like optical lenses and photography; and that it shared global leadership with the USA in electrical engineering and with the USA and Britain in mechanical engineering and steel. The USA and Germany had to some extent manufactured non-competitive engineering products because of the much lower German wage level. The war forced Germany to share leadership in chemicals and pharmaceuticals with the USA, and to cede it to the USA in mechanical engineering. I shall consider the chemical industry as a case study well documented by a good literature (Hayes, 1987; Plumpe, 1990).

In 1913 dyestuffs had formed 63 per cent of the turnover of the firms which in 1925 formed the I.G. Farben concern. The brilliant development, by BASF just before the war, of the Haber–Bosch process of ammonia synthesis enabled the large-scale development of a second main line of activity in the 1920s: artificial fertilisers, which by 1929 represented 44 per cent of turnover (dyestuffs having been reduced to 23 per cent). But this changing emphasis was an unfortunate one in two respects. British and US chemical firms stole the secrets of the process, thus eliminating I.G. Farben's **rent** on its invention. Despite this, Bosch, who became the founder chairman of I.G. Farben's management board, devoted 31 per cent of the firm's investment in plant and equipment to fertilisers. This merely added to rising excess world capacity in the industry, which in any case met the falling demand due to the world agricultural crisis of the later 1920s. Other great chemical firms were also affected – e.g. ICI's large investments at Billingham – but none was proportionately so committed to fertilisers as I.G. Farben.

The Haber–Bosch process had given I.G. Farben immense know-how in methods of high-pressure synthesis that it sought to exploit by applying it to the challenge of producing synthetic fuel oil from lignite. This swallowed up the greater part of I.G. Farben's research and development expenditure into new fields in the 1920s, but proved economically unviable when petroleum prices, instead of rising due to the expected exhaustion of natural oil fields, plummeted in the slump. Only the Benzin Contract of 1933 with the Third Reich – unforeseeable in the 1920s – created an interwar return on the research. At the same time I.G. Farben was committing substantial sums of money to the scarcely more successful research and development of synthetic rubber – even though the company only hoped to create a specialist niche-market product. This was also undercut by the collapse of natural rubber prices at the end of the 1920s. Another line of investment – in production facilities for artificial fibres – proved equally loss-making in the later 1920s because of cheap Italian competition.

In short, this study of I.G. Farben's research programme in the 1920s indicates much effort and technical ingenuity but little economic success. The future lay in fields to which the firm devoted comparatively slight resources: from much smaller budgets I.G. Farben laboratories invented PVC and polyurethane in the 1930s. Pharmaceuticals, too, were comparatively neglected.

This failure might indicate a sort of conservatism consistent with James' thesis of the entrepreneurial rigidity of middle-aged managers. The great projects relating to nitrogenous fertilisers, synthetic oil and rubber, and artificial fibres all pursued the recipe for success of the great dyestuffs revolution of the late nineteenth century – the replacement of specific non-renewable or apparently expensive natural products with similar synthetic substitutes, rather than looking for useful but all-new materials. However, US firms were simultaneously spending large sums on the oil-from-coal idea. I.G. Farben had not lost contact with the technological frontier. Its problem was divining where that frontier was next going to move. Perhaps what is really demonstrated by I.G. Farben's devotion to unsuccessful projects in the 1920s is the downside of German industry's faith in bigness. I.G. Farben was a German research and development monopoly in chemicals. For all its emphasis on intrafirm competition in research and development, its research priorities were, in the end, shaped by the 'technical vision' of one man – Carl Bosch. It was afflicted by the impossibility of predicting the truly new, which has ruined national technology policies.

Even so, I.G. Farben was not a commercial failure before the slump. It remained Germany's most export-orientated firm, 50 per cent of its production being exported in the later 1920s. What kept the firm afloat was the continued high profitability of dyestuffs. This rested partly on the exploitation of new markets – notably China, which became I.G. Farben's single largest export market in the 1920s – and on the innovation of new high-quality dyestuffs capable of defeating the fierce tariff barriers surrounding western markets. These profits financed the large research and development programme until the slump.

The success of the German electrical giants also rested on the further refinement of existing technologies (Feldenkirchen, 1999, pp. 69–96). They were slower to innovate consumer durables than their US counterparts (Dornseifer, 1995). The powerful postwar vision of 'rationalisation' focused on process rather than product innovation. In the nineteenth century the great German metalfabricating and engineering industries had focused on product design: how products were made, and how piece rates were set, had remained the province of experienced, shopfloor foremen (*Werkmeister*), and the rent from the sale of new products had made production efficiency of secondary importance. Interest in 'production engineering', especially in the ideas of 'Taylorism' had developed just before the war. A major preoccupation in Germany became the reorganisation of shopfloor tasks and layouts with a view to minimising work time (for the following see Homburg, 1978, 1991; Stollberg, 1981; von Freyberg, 1989; Nolan, 1994). After the war and especially the stabilisation interest quickened.

But most German plant-level rationalisation stopped short of 'Fordism' – of mechanised, moving assembly-line methods of manufacture. Fordist methods were potentially applicable to many assembling processes, but above all to the machining and assembly of metal fabricates. As the manufacture of metal goods – from cutlery to steel ships – had been central to German industrial advance before 1914, Fordism was a major challenge to German industry. The low real wages of the inflation period temporarily insulated Germany from US competition. At Siemens, the modernisation of intraworks transportation, which had been stimulated immediately after the war by the relative rise of unskilled wages, was suspended as wage levels plummeted in 1922–3. Only after 1924 did the vogue for 'Fordism' take centre-stage in the business and technical press, expressing the perceived need to 'catch-up' with the US. Numerous Germans made pilgrimages to Ford's plants in Detroit. After such a tour Carl Köttgen, a leading Siemens director who also directed the Reich Agency for Efficiency, published in 1925 a book called *Das wirtschaftliche Amerika* ('Business Efficiency in America') which popularised the advantages of Fordist methods in Germany (though it also noted the problems). Yet even in Siemens in the later 1920s only a few hundred workers worked fully machine-paced assembly lines (mainly assembling vacuum cleaners!), although a few thousand more were working on self-paced assembly lines. In this attenuated sense, presumably, a questionnaire of the German Metal-Workers Union in 1930 reported that one-sixth of car and electro-technical plants, but less than one-twelfth of clock-making, precision engineering, optical and machine-building firms had adopted assembly line methods. Among car-makers only the largest – Opel (soon to be taken over by General Motors) – introduced full machine-paced assembly line manufacture.

In other industries the record was variable, but there were some notable examples of non-assembly-line process innovation – in coal mining, in iron and steel processes and in plate glass. The Ruhr coal cartel was also involved in oil-from-coal research and trying to pioneer long-distance gas transmission to ease its marketing problems.

The above account suggests a restraint on German business investment apart from wage pressure – one already stated in Köttgen's book. Automated assembly line methods reduced costs only at a large-scale of production. But in German conditions there was a contradiction between production efficiency – which demanded such economies of scale – and business efficiency, which required instant adjustment of product quantities and product designs to abruptly changing market conditions (James, 1986, p. 153). The sudden economic recession of 1925–6, just as the 'Fordist' enthusiasm was taking hold, underlined this truth. Even less calculable was export demand. German industry's access to export markets depended on other countries' tariff policies, which were now rendered so much less calculable than before the war by the brittleness of the postwar European political system. The classic 'Fordist' technology, involving fully mechanised assembly lines on which semi-skilled labour operated highly task-specific machine tools, had nothing of the versatility required by German market conditions. 'Catch-up' required not only adoption, but also adaptation of new technologies to specific market and factor-cost conditions. Adaptation took time and was still experimental in the 1920s, involving product innovation in the German machine tool industry. Instead German industry devised flexible quasi-assembly lines, such as 'serial' production which sequenced machine tool location so as to minimise transport of the workpiece. Not until the 1930s were the design problems sufficiently solved, and did technology reach a sufficient 'stasis' in the German context, for widespread implementation of machine-paced assembly lines.

In Germany, unlike in the UK, there was no ingrained resistance from skilled labour towards new technology. The Marxist ideology of the German Metal-Workers Union embraced technical progress as the solution to human poverty and as tending, by the contradiction it set up between 'production efficiency' and 'market efficiency', to accelerate the era when a democratic state would proceed to socialist planning. The 'German' path to mass production did not involve a general 'deskilling' in the German machine-building and electrical industries. This stood post-1945 Germany in good stead. Not until the end of the slump did the Metal-Workers Union begin to view 'rationalisation' primarily for its job-destroying implications (Broadberry and Wagner, 1996).

We might, then, hypothesise that productivity advance was impeded in Germany in the 1920s by Germany's loss of unchallenged technological leadership in some areas and the time taken to adapt to the new competitive environment that loss of patent rights, loss of research and development initiative and the challenge of US mass production technologies now placed her in. Evidently the uncertainty of the new global competitive environment was felt by all the participating great firms and, as already stated, they sought to reduce the risks and protect the return on their research and development investments by far more extensive international cartelisation and market-sharing agreements than had existed before 1914. This hypothesis suggests that the inflationary environment did nothing to assist innovation and catch-up. It is not inconsistent with the Borchardt hypothesis regarding a profits squeeze, but neither is it dependent on it.

German agriculture remained technically isolated, largely unmechanised and backward in this era. The reconnection to global agricultural prices in 1924 exposed it to the fall in these prices from 1925, and the 1925 tariff legislation, which re-enacted the specific duties of 1906 at generally higher price levels, was inadequate to restore profitability. Yet it re-accumulated debt after 1924 at an amazing rate. From 1929 German agricultural tariff levels rose markedly (James, 1986, pp. 246ff; Braun, 1990, pp. 54–6).

# 5
# The slump

## The course and causes of the slump in Germany, 1928–1931

The slump started early in Germany (though not earlier than in many primary-product exporting nations), well before the Wall Street crash of October 1929. It became more severe in Germany than in any other industrial nation, probably even than in the USA. A striking feature of the German slump was the continuous improvement of the balance of visible and invisible trade with abroad (net of reparations) from mid-1927 to spring 1931, even although German exports began to decline from mid-1929 (see Table 5.1). German tariffs on agricultural products rose appreciably in this period; but even all other classes of imports fell faster at current prices than the corresponding export classes (Hoffmann *et al.*, 1965, pp. 520, 524). This suggests that aggregate domestic demand for goods and services was declining faster in Germany than in the rest of the world in this period. This decline centred on domestic investment and State spending, and so explanation of the German slump hinges on explaining these. The suggestion that it commenced in consumer demand arises from failure to distinguish reduced business investment in stocks of consumer goods from reduced final sales.

From the summer of 1931 the global and German financial crises and the sterling devaluation impacted on German home demand but even more on export demand, so that the German export surplus began to shrink. These vice-like pressures on German demand drove unemployment to unimaginable levels in 1932 (James, 1986, pp. 283f; Stachura, 1986; Evans and Geary, 1987).

Table 5.1. The German balance of payments 1925–33 (figures in millions of reichsmarks)[1]

| | 1925 | 1926 | 1927 | 1928 | 1929 | 1930 | 1931 | 1932 | 1933 |
|---|---|---|---|---|---|---|---|---|---|
| **Goods and services account** | | | | | | | | | |
| Exports of goods/services | 9937 | 11179 | 11876 | 13424 | 14882 | 13309 | 10856 | 6997 | 5692 |
| Reparations in kind[2] | 665 | 724 | 784 | 838 | 1007 | 707 | 393 | 0 | 0 |
| Imports of goods/services | −12584 | −10578 | −14975 | −14901 | −15221 | −11920 | −8021 | −5680 | −4713 |
| Balance of trade | −1982 | 1325 | −2315 | −639 | 668 | 2096 | 3228 | 1317 | 979 |
| Interest balance | −6 | −173 | −345 | −563 | −800 | −1000 | −1200 | −900 | −698 |
| Reparations cash transfers | −1057 | −1191 | −1584 | −1990 | −2337 | −1706 | −988 | −160 | 0 |
| Total current a/c balance | −3045 | −39 | −4244 | −3192 | −2469 | −610 | 1040 | 257 | 281 |
| **Capital account** | | | | | | | | | |
| Capital exports | −87 | −118 | −854 | −2852 | −2119 | −2442 | −3160 | −1299 | −1410 |
| Capital imports | 1518 | 1641 | 4336 | 5975 | 3544 | 3678 | 3817 | 550 | 603 |
| Capital balance: | 1431 | 1523 | 3482 | 3123 | 1425 | 1236 | 657 | −749 | −807 |
| **Balance items** | | | | | | | | | |
| Gold/foreign exchange | −90 | −568 | 452 | −931 | 165 | 120 | 1706 | 233 | 447 |
| Residual | 1704 | −916 | 310 | 1000 | 879 | −746 | −3403 | 259 | 79 |

1 In this table transactions requiring the acquisition of foreign currency have a minus sign; transactions acquiring it, and reparations deliveries in kind, have a plus sign. Thus the 1704 m reichsmark residual for 1925 implies that Germany must have either had export earnings or capital imports in excess of those shown to meet the apparent overall deficit in the balance.
2 Exports of goods and services free to the recipient Allied country, the exporter being reimbursed by the German government.

*Source:* Ritschl (in press).

Recorded unemployment in mid-1929, at 1.5m, was only 200,000 higher than in mid-1928, as export growth had offset domestic recession. It reached 3m in mid-1930, and peaked at 6m in the first months of 1932 (Balderston, 1993, p. 2). Probably a further 2m unemployed were invisible to the statistics because, by choice or administrative decision, they were no longer registered as job-seekers. This may be inferred from the 2m drop in the recorded labour force (recorded employed plus recorded unemployed) between 1929 and 1932. In Britain, by contrast, the recorded labour force increased during the slump. On British definitions total German industrial unemployment, visible and invisible, probably exceeded 40 per cent in 1932 (British unemployment was 23 per cent), and was probably significantly greater than US unemployment (Figure 5.1). The threat of unemployment spared virtually no-one. German salary earners were far more liable to unemployment than their British counterparts, even if less liable than German wage earners. German unemployment was spread far more equally across industries and regions than British (Table 5.3). Germany did have structurally depressed industries – in the form of the so-called 'speciality' export industries, such as musical instruments, clocks and watches, cutlery, tools and toys, whose prewar success had rested on varying

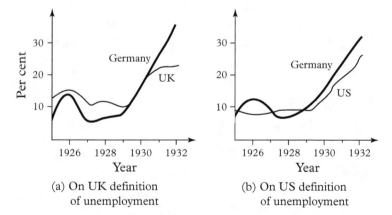

(a) On UK definition of unemployment

(b) On US definition of unemployment

Figure 5.1   Comparative unemployment Germany/UK and Germany/US 1925–32 (by per cent). (a) on UK definition of unemployment and (b) on US definition of unemployment. From Balderston, 1993, pp. 9, 13.

Table 5.2. Selected German macroeconomic series 1925–33 (figures in millions of reichsmarks)

| Year | 1 GNP at factor cost[1] | 2 Private consumption | 3 Private investment | 4 Investment in stocks | 5 Public spending on goods and services | 6 Public investment | 7 Public transfer payments | 8 Reparations burden | 9 Balance of trade and interest payments |
|---|---|---|---|---|---|---|---|---|---|
| 1925 | 71145 | 53629 | 8905 | 1320 | 9279 | 1407 | 8199 | 1080 | −1988 |
| 1926 | 73657 | 55394 | 8390 | −830 | 9550 | 2285 | 8253 | 1297 | 1152 |
| 1927 | 82821 | 61551 | 10280 | 2380 | 11273 | 2690 | 9561 | 1712 | −2660 |
| 1928 | 88486 | 66295 | 11020 | 1310 | 11064 | 2658 | 8905 | 2159 | −1202 |
| 1929 | 88448 | 65923 | 10120 | 360 | 12181 | 2670 | 10217 | 1964 | −132 |
| 1930 | 81935 | 63507 | 8280 | −1740 | 10794 | 2092 | 8915 | 1879 | 1096 |
| 1931 | 67953 | 55274 | 4980 | −3130 | 8799 | 1456 | 7811 | 988 | 2028 |
| 1932 | 55544 | 45309 | 3130 | −1520 | 8208 | 1095 | 8025 | 183 | 417 |
| 1933 | 57026 | 43195 | 3650 | 440 | 9462 | 1416 | 9313 | 149 | 281 |

1 The sum of cols. 2, 3, 4, 5 and 9. Col. 6 is incl. in col. 5. Cols. 7 & 8 are tax financed transfers out of GNP.
2 Sums raised in reichsmarks by taxation, special levies on enterprises, or borrowing. Differs from sums transferred (Table 5.1).
Source: Ritschl (in press).

Table 5.3. Industry-specific unemployment in Germany
and the UK, June 1933

| Industry | Rate of unemployment (%) | |
| --- | --- | --- |
|  | Germany | UK |
| Coal mining | 33.1 | 37.4 |
| Sand and stone | 38.8 | 21.5 |
| Glass, ceramics | 35.6 | 21.5 |
| Iron, steel-making | 41.9 | 38.8 |
| Machine building | 48.9 | 27.3 |
| Small metal wares | 42.3 | 20.2 |
| Shipbuilding | 63.5 | 61.1 |
| Vehicles, aircraft | 39.7 | 17.1 |
| Electrical | 41.9 | 14.8 |
| Precision instruments and optical | 32.1 | 12.5 |
| Chemicals | 25.6 | 12.7 |
| Textiles | 24.3 | 20.4 |
| Leather, clothing | 23.6 | 10.9 |
| Woodworking | 43.6 | 18.3 |
| Musical instruments and toys | 55.1 | 20.1 |
| Food, drink, tobacco | 25.8 | 11.9 |
| Rubber, asbestos | 31.9 | 13.6 |
| Papermaking | 23.9 | 8.5 |
| Paper wares | 31.1 | 8.3 |
| Printing, publishing | 27.1 | 9.4 |
| Building, public works | 52.3 | 25.4 |
| Water, gas, electricity | 15.2 | 10.2 |
| Transport, excl. railway | 29.9 | 21.3 |
| Distribution | 28.8 | 11.3 |
| Commerce, banks, insurance | 11.4 | 4.7 |
| Catering trades | 28.5 | 14 |
| Entertainment and recreation | 40.9 | 19.4 |
| Professions | 16.7 | 5.4 |
| Total shown | 34.4 | 19.5 |

*Source:* Balderston (1993), p. 3.

combinations of low wages and skill; and of course agriculture was a structurally depressed activity. But the unemployment of the German slump was unambiguously **cyclical**, and it is to the recession of aggregate demand, and especially of aggregate domestic demand, that we must look to explain it.

The dominant explanations centre on the role of the capital markets. The direct cost effects of rising real wages did not cause the downturn, even though they may have reduced investment demand (Broadberry and Ritschl, 1994, p. 25).

Economic historiography traditionally explained recession in Germany in 1928–9 as the backwash of the US stock market boom of 1928–9 (Schmidt, 1934; Kindleberger, 1973, pp. 70ff, 116f). This US boom centred on common stocks (equities, shares) and the sale of both US and non-US bonds on Wall Street languished during the boom (Balderston, 1993, pp. 455f). German firms made few or no share issues on Wall Street. German short-term interest rates, too, were affected by the very high short rates that could be earned on stock market loans in New York. German share prices in Berlin fell rather than rose. The German equity market had experienced its own 'black Friday' on 13 May 1927, more than $2^{1}/_{2}$ years before Wall Street's 'black Thursday', due to an inept attempt of Reichsbank President Schacht to dampen 'speculation' (Balderston, 1993, pp. 207ff). What is more interesting is that German equity prices continued to decline irregularly thereafter, during the Wall Street boom. Although there was German resistance to the idea of selling German equity to foreigners the more likely reason is global pessimism regarding German economic 'fundamentals', congruent with the decline in business investment intentions from late 1927 (Voth, forthcoming).

Arguing, from a Keynesian stance, that monetary forces did not cause the great depression, Temin argued that the earliest signs of falling aggregate demand in Germany occurred in investment in stocks of goods, which was insensitive to interest-rate changes (Temin, 1971). Thus he argued that the German recession was independent of the Wall Street boom. However perhaps the best evidence for this independence lies in the monetary sphere, in the rise of German interest rates relative to US rates from the second half of 1927 (see above p. 65). German capital market conditions worsened not just because of the Wall St boom or slump.

Ritschl (1998) argues that lenders became increasingly nervous about the repayability of the rising German commercial debt to abroad, given the rising German reparations payments schedule under the Dawes Plan. Schacht's campaign against foreign borrowing by the municipalities, no doubt actuated by these anxieties (McNeil, 1986, pp. 135–95), would itself tend to aggravate them. On top of this, premonitions of a revision of the Dawes Plan to reduce transfer protection (as actually happened in the Young Plan) would unsettle foreign lenders and cause them to mark up their loan offer rates. Finally, this theory might also imply that the prospect of the end of the Dawes Plan would act as an incentive to borrowers, especially long-term borrowers, to borrow sooner rather than later, whilst the transfer clause lasted. But on the other hand the known provisionality of the Dawes Plan might increase lender preference for short-term loans. Such a dynamic would explain the frenetic pace of German foreign bond borrowing in 1928 despite rising interest rates and increasing placement difficulties on Wall Street.

Balderston argued that it was signs of the Reich reverting to deficitary fiscal management that unsettled the markets. Whilst in fiscal years 1924–5 and 1925–6 the Reich's current income from taxation, etc. had exceeded its expenditures, from 1926–7 current income fell significantly below expenditure. The proceeds of the large surplus of 1924–5, plus the large **seignorage** gains from the reissue of the coinage, could be covertly used to more or less defray these deficits until the end of 1927–8. But in the longer run the fact that the larger part of direct tax revenues was transferred to the federal states and municipalities made the Reich's retained revenues inelastic (Balderston, 1993, pp. 231–50; James, 1986, pp. 43–59). From mid-1927 the Agent-General for Reparations, one of whose prime duties was to report to the Allies on the soundness of German fiscal management, began publicly to criticise the profligacy of German public finance. One source of his anxiety could have been the serious undersubscription of a domestic bond issue of the Reich in February 1927 – the first such issue since the stabilisation (McNeil, 1986, pp. 143ff). The bond issue was to consolidate debts incurred through a (perhaps less-than-fully controlled) experiment in fiscal reflation the previous autumn (McNeil, 1986, pp. 125–33; Balderston, 1993, pp. 224–5; Clingan, 2001, pp. 72–88). This undersubscription could have meant that, in the future, similarly unfundable Reich borrowing requirements would have to be monetised by the Reichsbank, thus threatening the gold standard. Reparations and almost all foreign loans were denominated in foreign currencies and their value was not directly affected by a devaluation of the reichsmark. But the threat of devaluation might precipitate a flight from the mark on the part of reichsmark asset holders, thus causing a transfer crisis.

These Germano-centric explanations may help to explain why German borrowing in the US failed to revive following the Wall Street crash. US domestic bond borrowing revived in 1930 and Germany's surplus on current transactions was growing throughout 1929–31, as we have seen. Ritschl (1998) argues that the Young Plan deterred further foreign lending to Germany by seriously curtailing German 'transfer protection'. Against this theory it might be observed that the interest-rate differential between Berlin and New York narrowed from January to September 1930 (see Figure 4.1 p. 63), and that what seemed to frighten investors in Germany most was not the prospect of reparations being paid, but ominous signs that they might not be paid. The German banks experienced three periods of crisis withdrawal of deposits to abroad in this period – in April–May 1929, in September–October 1930 and in May–July 1931. The first of these was associated with the threat of a breakdown in the Paris negotiations, which (subsequently) produced the Young Plan. This breakdown was provoked by Schacht's demands (see p. 25). It was the fear that Germany would not accept the Allied reparations terms, not the realisation that she would, that triggered this financial crisis. The major cause of the second crisis was the shocking rise in the Nazi Reichstag representation in the elections of 14 September – and the Nazis had gained public recognition by agitating against the Young Plan. Among the many precipitants of the third and worst crisis was a 'Reparations Declaration' by Brüning, which seemed to presage a further German revision attempt (James, 1986, pp. 284, 302). James argued that the high-tax regime of post-stabilisation Germany retarded German growth. This encouraged foreign borrowing (especially by municipalities hampered by sluggish tax revenues), but also triggered political protest, which ultimately unsettled the foreign lenders (James, 1986, p. 108). Hence Ritschl's explanation must compete with a different explanation for fears of a transfer crisis – the right-wing shift in German domestic politics, and foreign investors' consequent fears of being 'held hostage' by Germany in its effort to extract reparations concessions from the Allies (see p. 24). In fact, a synthesis of the two views might best explain the appalling instability of Germany's capital account with abroad during the slump: for foreign investors were in a cleft stick – whether Germany chose to pay or not to pay reparations, their investments were insecure.

These various explanations of the cessation of German foreign borrowing agree that it had a severely deflationary effect on German aggregate demand, above all on infrastructural investment and on (other) government spending. Balderston (1993, pp. 382f) argued further that an inexplicably deepening business pessimism, affecting industrial and commercial investment, aggravated the depression, perhaps driving it during 1930 when the German–US interest-rate gap actually narrowed. The role of cartels in maintaining prices and therefore converting deflationary forces into output and employment declines was emphasised by Petzina (1969). If wages had fallen as fast as prices, unemployment would have been smaller, but since wage contracts are less flexible than most prices (especially food prices), worker resistance to wage cuts is explicable and normal in slumps.

### The banking crisis

There are excellent narratives in English of the German banking crisis of 1931 (Kindleberger, 1973; James, 1984; Brown, 1988; Feldman, 1995). It began in May, apparently following news of the collapse of the Austrian Credit Anstalt (Schubert, 1991); accelerated in June, apparently following Brüning's 'Reparations Declaration' of 5 June (see p. 84); and reached its dénouement with a general closure of bank counters between 13 July and early August, following news that one of the great banks, the DANAT, was insolvent because of the catastrophic losses of one of its main borrowers, the Nordwolle textile concern. The accelerating withdrawal of deposits involved large demands for foreign exchange. The banks refinanced their foreign-currency losses at the Reichsbank, threatening to reduce its foreign reserves below the statutory minimum ratio of 40 percent of the note issue. To avoid this and its potentially disastrous effect on confidence in the gold standard, Luther (who replaced Schacht as Reichsbank President between February 1930 and March 1933), eventually took the standard step of seeking foreign-currency credits from foreign central banks. The Federal Reserve Bank of New York put pressure on Luther to ration bill discounts – as in 1924 – in order to limit the commercial banks' demands on the Reichsbank's foreign reserves and instead liquidate their own. Rationing was initiated on 24 June, and hastened the collapse of the DANAT bank (James, 1985). In previous crises, especially that of 1930, the German banks had been able to refinance themselves at foreign correspondent banks; but whilst these banks did not rush to withdraw their credits in 1931, they showed no willingness to extend them (James, 1986, pp. 303). The offer of a French loan in July was conditional on renunciation of the Austro-German customs union project and of attempts to renegotiate the Young Plan, and Brüning rated the domestic political risk of such undertakings too high (James, 1986, pp. 313f; Ferguson and Temin, 2001). The banking crisis was not confined to the Berlin great banks, nor just to commercial banks, but engulfed the large German public-sector banking sector (chiefly savings banks) as well, chiefly because of their large-scale lending to near-insolvent municipalities (James, 1986, pp. 101ff).

In an immediate sense the cause of any banking crisis is panic deposit withdrawals – i.e. action by the banks' *creditors*. But is their panic to be regarded as a final cause, or was it prompted by justifiable fears regarding the liquidity or solvency of the banks – fears regarding the banks' *assets* and *debtors*?

Traditional historiography (Born, 1983, pp. 257–68) regarded foreign deposits as inherently less stable than domestic deposits and so blamed the crisis largely on the presence of this large body of unreliable deposits in the German banking system. Once the banks had become so dependent on foreign deposits in the mid-1920s, a crisis was only a matter of time. But from the perspective of the huge global short capital flows of the end of the twentieth century, the instability of foreign deposits itself needs to be explained. Indeed, it is not even certain that foreign deposits were less stable than domestic. James argued that the run in 1931 started with the withdrawal of domestically owned deposits (James, 1986, pp. 298–303).

The historiography has also blamed the quality of bank assets, as precipitating depositor nervousness. The banks already had many bad and frozen loans at the advent of the 1931 crisis, and irrecoverable municipal debt threatened the public-sector banks. James emphasises the unusual conjuncture of bad private-sector and public-sector debts due to the fiscal crisis: usually in depressions the value of public debt appreciates as nominal interest rates fall. (James, 1984; 1986, pp. 284f.) But were the banks culpable? Macroeconomic changes outside any reasonable foresight could have made sound business judgements of the later 1920s into disasters in the early 1930s (Voth, 2000). Undeniably, however, the reduction in the ratio of own to borrowed capital which the banks permitted for competitive reasons in the later 1920s (see p. 63) made bank solvency much more vulnerable to bad debts.

Against such 'business-of-banking' explanations of the crisis stands the fact that the 1931 crisis was the last and most virulent of the three episodes of bank withdrawals, and the previous two – in 1929 and 1930 – had not been associated with bad news about bank assets, but with potentially bad news about reparations (pp. 84). In all three episodes bank-deposit withdrawals entailed the purchase of foreign currency, suggesting that fear of currency restrictions might have been a common element. The possibility that a German government (especially a right-wing one) might hold deposits hostage in an effort to extract better reparations terms cannot have escaped deposit-holders. The three episodes also coincided with news of fiscal crises (in 1930 both the deposit declines and deseasonalised losses of Reichsbank reserves actually started in July) and Balderston (1993, pp. 139, 451) argued that such news also weakened confidence in the currency. Ferguson and Temin (2001) connect both the fiscal and the currency crisis to the customs union project and the reparations démarche, which stemmed a potentially stabilising flow of French capital.

Stabilising the German banking sector when it reopened after the 'bank holidays' of the second half of July required the imposition of currency controls from 15 July alongside a (temporarily) very high Reichsbank discount rate. The currency controls limited the foreign-currency servicing of German foreign bonds. As they were subsequently tightened foreign bondholders in the end lost the greater part of their investments. Foreign banks were exempted from such controls on their loans to German banks, because their goodwill was vital to future German foreign trade. Instead, 'standstill' agreements with them were finalised in September. Originally expected to last six months, they were successively renegotiated throughout the 1930s, and foreign banks eventually secured the repayment of most of the German banks' engagements to them (James, 1986, pp. 314ff).

As regards domestic financial stabilisation, the banks' *illiquidity* – largely their shortage of 'eligible paper' for rediscounting at the Reichsbank – was solved by arrangements for indirectly relaxing the Reichsbank's rediscount criteria, and by its relaxation, from now on, of its 40 per cent note cover restriction. The great banks' *solvency* was eventually restored by greater or lesser injections of Reich capital – supplied not as cash but as treasury paper.

Even with proactive bill rediscounting and modest monetary expansion on the part of the Reichsbank (James, 1985a, pp. 287ff) Berlin market discount rates in later 1931 and 1932 were never less than 3½ per cent above New York rates and the reichsmark was weak. This suggests that the still-live threat of capital flight, evading the still-imperfect currency controls, continued to limit the Reichsbank's freedom of action. Given expected price declines in excess of 5 per cent, per annum, the nominal market discount rates of more than 5 per cent from June 1931 to May 1932 implied 'real' discount rates above 10 percent. This, plus the banks' evident efforts to liquidate unsound advances, forced business to destock on a massive scale. The instability of the banks aggravated the Reich's fiscal crisis in 1931–2 (see pp. 95–8). This financial vice, squeezing the German economy, plus the effects of maintaining the German exchange rate when sterling depreciated after September 1931, were the domestic causes of the business and employment catastrophe of 1931–2 (James, 1986, pp. 285–91, 323; Balderston, 1993, 388).

## Fiscal policy in the German slump

The German slump is best known for its 'perversely' restrictive fiscal policy, usually associated with Heinrich Brüning, chancellor from 30 March 1930 to 30 May 1932, though it originated with the preceding government (James, 1986, p. 58). In actuality the budget was in deficit throughout the slump, not of course because of deliberate policy, but because of the contractionary effects of the recession on tax revenues and its expansionary effects on welfare expenditures.

It is common to try to isolate the effects of deliberate budget policy on aggregate demand by calculating what the budgetary balance implicit in the tax and spending regime would have been at full employment. Unquestionably the effect of the tax and spending policy changes of the slump years would, at full employment, have moved the budget dramatically into surplus – i.e. fiscal policy became dramatically more deflationary (Cohn, 1997). These changes affected aggregate demand mainly through the catastrophic knock-on effects on local authorities' spending on goods, services and welfare of the curtailment of tax transfers from the Reich, unassuaged by any possibility of further borrowing (James, 1986, pp. 97–108).

Stabilisation of the Reich's finances was indeed Brüning's foremost political aim. Reich President von Hindenburg had placed the presidential powers of emergency decree at his disposal if he could not obtain parliamentary consent for fiscal reform. Brüning did, with difficulty, persuade the Reichstag to pass the spring 1930 budget, which obtained DNVP support by adding agricultural protectionist measures to a variant of those on which the previous administration had fallen (Patch, 1998, pp. 78–81). But as soon as the budget was passed, news of declines in revenues and increases in expenditure due to the worsening recession caused him to seek further tax increases. Brüning's proposal of a special tax on civil servants, company directors and persons in private professions alienated the DVP, whilst a proposed local authority poll tax alienated the SPD. After the Reichstag finally rejected his measures on 16 July 1930, Brüning enacted them by emergency decree the next day. On the 18th the Reichstag used its constitutional powers to annul this decree retrospectively. Brüning dissolved the Reichstag, called a general election for 14 September and re-enacted virtually the same measures by a second decree on 26 July. Brüning could probably have balanced the budget by parliamentary methods if he had placated the SPD rather than the DVP – but Hindenburg had appointed him to avoid such a dependence on socialists (Meister, 1991, pp. 186–9; Clingan, 2001, pp. 171–81).

This set the scene for Brüning's administration. He followed up his electoral reverse of 14 September by pushing on with his financial programme. He promulgated four great Presidential 'Decrees for Securing the German Economy and Finances', on 1 December 1930, 5 June, 6 October and 8 December 1931. The so-called

Dietramzell Decree of 24 August 1931 gave the states extensive powers to force budgetary balance on local authorities. It was when Hindenburg refused to countersign a fifth deflationary decree at the end of May 1932 that Brüning resigned. The four decrees centred on tax increases, social benefit cuts and expenditure cuts. Decree IV (8 December 1931) also included comprehensive regulations reducing cartel prices, collectively-contracted wages and interest rates. Attempts at consensual price and wage reduction had failed in the summer of 1930, when lack of wider business and political support had frustrated the efforts of some business leaders, supported by Brüning, to breathe life into a new 'co-operative partnership' with the trade unions. The Brüning government consistently sought to negotiate price reductions in return for supporting wage reductions. In fact the draconian provisions of Decree IV aroused amazingly little organised opposition (Patch, 1998, pp. 84–6, 110f, 115f, 212f).

Whilst Brüning was thus earning his reputation as the 'hunger chancellor', the policy ideas of the Keynesian revolution were 'in the making' in Germany as well as in Cambridge (James, 1986, pp. 324ff). In January 1931 the government itself had appointed a Commission under the former Minister of Labour, Heinrich Brauns, to recommend anti-unemployment measures (Ministry of Labour, 1931). Its Second Report of June 1931 had recommended a public works programme financed by a foreign loan (Ministry of Labour, 1931) but the banking crisis put paid to foreign financing. In mid-September 1931 a 'confidential conference' of economists and interested government officials met in the Reichsbank building to discuss possibilities of bank-financed and Reichsbank-supported credit reflation in Germany (though there is no evidence of Luther supporting such ideas), on the basis of a paper on the subject by an official in the Reich Business Affairs Ministry, Wilhelm Lautenbach (Borchardt and Schötz, 1991). This paper proposed a wage cut whose effect on purchasing power and aggregate demand would be offset by simultaneous State public works projects to be financed by commercial bank loans facilitated by Reichsbank rediscount guarantees. This two-pronged policy would reduce wages relative to prices, prompt employers to hire more labour, and thus kickstart the economy into recovery. The hope was that this recovery would then enable repayment of 'frozen' loans that were immobilising the banking system, enabling further extensions of credit. At that time the State Secretary (i.e. the civil service head) of the Reich Finance Ministry, Hans Schäffer, composed a 'position paper' expressing views remarkably open to such reasoning. In early 1932 Ernst Wagemann, Director of the Reich Statistical Office as well as of the semi-official Institute for Business Cycle Research produced a plan intended to cut the link between the bank/'giral' money used as means of payment, and the currently ruinous loan portfolios of the banks. The socialist trade unions published the 'Woytinsky–Tarnow–Baade' Plan for public works-based reflation in January 1932, though it failed to receive the endorsement of the SPD (Patch, 1998, pp. 201–4, 216f, 260f; Barkai pp. 56f).

This plethora of plans gave intellectual backbone to mounting criticism of Brüning's deflationary course, not just outside, but even inside the cabinet. The Minister of Business Affairs whom he appointed in October 1931, Professor H. Warmbold (a former I.G. Farben executive) supported expansionary policies and almost resigned in the run-up to the Fourth Emergency Decree of December 1931. The Finance and Labour Ministers, Dietrich and Stegerwald, supported deflation with very sore consciences. Cabinet resistance to continued deflation mounted in spring 1932 (Patch, 1998, pp. 204, 210f, 217, 259f). After Brüning himself left office at the end of May, the verdict of history turned immediately against him. The apparently stunning success of Nazi employment policies seems to vindicate retrospectively the analogous plans of the 'reformers' of 1931–2 (Overy, 1996; though see James, 1986, pp. 343–419). A 'Keynesian' consensus emerged amongst historians of economic policy: Brüning was culpable in choosing deflation when he could and should have chosen reflation, and his choice immiserised Germany and opened the floodgates to Nazism.

Why did Brüning do it? One strain of historiography stemming from these 'reformers' blames Brüning himself for intellectual boneheadness and perhaps personality defects. He didn't understand or sympathise with the 'new economics' (Clingan, 2001). However, Finance Minister Reinhold's attempt at fiscal reflation in 1926 had already given Germany a tutorial in this subject (Meister, 1991, pp. 168f). Brüning came into office in spring 1930 promoting an extensive work creation programme that was to supplement his budgetary reforms (Balderston, 1993, pp. 296ff). And he claimed to be planning to revive this programme once reparations were abolished, but to have been dismissed '100 metres before the goal' (Patch, 1998, p. 261).

To political historians, politics explains all, and especially from the 1960s they mostly argued that Brüning was rational but misguided: he subordinated fiscal policy to reparations policy (Helbich, 1962; Meister, 1991, pp. 395ff). To some historians this was wanton, cold-blooded pursuit of 'prestige policy' at the expense of the millions of unemployed. His own *Memoirs*, published posthumously but mainly written shortly after he left office, suggest the more sympathetic motivation, that he viewed reparations and war debts as the cause of the world and German slump; so that his reparations policy was in part an economic policy of the long run. The end of reparations would open the doors to fresh borrowing abroad and would produce a healthier world economy as a market for German exports. He therefore needed to win Allied consent to the abolition of reparations. To secure this, he sought to show them Germany's incapacity to pay by a new and scrupulous 'fulfilment policy' – by balancing the budget at all costs – the action which the Allies required as proof of the sincerity of German compliance. The price- and wage-cutting elements of the Fourth Emergency Decree were of a piece with this: they were designed to bring home to the Allies that Germany could only pay – and if the Allies did not relent, would certainly only pay – by exporting unemployment to them. Moreover, after the elections of September 1930, Brüning could implicitly threaten the Allies with unilateral abrogation by Germany: if he failed, the right – Hugenberg and Hitler – stood in the wings. Deploying a Keynesian view of the 'multiplier effects' of balancing the budget in a depression, historians argued that the more Brüning's fiscal and price-level policies plunged Germany into misery, the better they served his purpose, by displaying the human cost to Germany of Allied obduracy (Sanmann, 1965).

Another historiography emphasised the ulterior domestic objectives of deflation. Brüning, acting in the interests of business, 'instrumentalised' fiscal policy in order to worsen the slump and weaken the trade unions and the SPD – the bulwark of the Weimar constitution. Thus he sought to shape an economic environment in which the basic Weimar 'labourist' compromises over wage and social policy could be repudiated and replaced by a free, individualistic labour market and minimalist social-service state; and in which the political constitution could be revised in an authoritarian direction (Witt, 1982a; Weisbrod, 1990, pp. 52ff). His reparations policy could also be explained on the grounds of his political need to outflank the right.

Brüning certainly cut back social welfare and viewed the wage level as excessive. His Fourth Emergency Decree of December 1931 cut basic wages to the level of early 1927 (James, 1986, pp. 67ff). But he supported his Labour Minister, the long-time Catholic trade-union leader Adam Stegerwald, in resisting the strident demand of the great business associations for abolition of the collective-wage-contract system and compulsory arbitration (Balderston, 1993, p. 46; Patch, 1998, p. 172).

The three explanations just given of Brüning's economic policies – intellectual ignorance, instrumentalisation of fiscal policy in the service of reparations policy, and/or in the service of domestic economic and political restructuring – agree that Brüning was culpable in choosing deflation, because he could have chosen reflation. They require a flanking political explanation of how Brüning, despite his parliamentary weakness, could consistently persuade the Reichstag not to rescind his emergency decrees. He relied after September 1930 on SPD 'toleration' for fear of something worse – a right-wing dictatorship. At times he used the threat against the SPD that if it failed to support him, then Brüning's own party (Centre) would pull the plug on the long-standing SPD-led coalition that governed Prussia (Patch, 1998, p.164).

The consensus blaming Brüning was challenged by Borchardt in 1978/9 (Borchardt, 1991) when he argued that Brüning simply had no 'room for manoeuvre' to do other than deflate. Borchardt argued this on five main points. Firstly, no-one could have foreseen the severity of the slump until summer 1931, and by then it was too late to take measures to prevent the 6m unemployment of early 1932. Secondly, there was no political support for reflation. Thirdly, even the wildest plans of the economic expansionists of 1931–2 were far too modest (by realistic assessments of their 'multiplier effects') to more than slightly dent the huge mass of unemployment, and fourthly, such policies would have been impossible to finance.

Fifthly, reflation would have solved nothing: the economy was 'sick' anyway, and would sooner or later have produced a slump (this argument was discussed in chapter 4).

These arguments unleashed a controversy that spilled over into the German quality press in the early 1980s, partly, at least, because they challenged the comfortable view that if only Brüning had acted more sensibly, Germany could have been spared the whole Hitler nightmare. The first of Borchardt's points was generally conceded; namely, that contemporaries viewed the slump in its early stages through the lens of the current vogue for business cycle theories. These treated slumps as quite rapid correctives of monetary or real 'disproportionalities' (given price and wage flexibility). Only following the banking crisis did more pessimistic prognostications gain ground (Meister, 1991, pp. 131ff; James, 1986, pp. 324–30). So the debate has come to centre on whether Brüning could have switched to reflation from the summer of 1931.

Borchardt's second point was conceded in economic but not political terms. True, the scale of contemporary plans was inadequate to the crisis, but if the government had only been seen to be combating the crisis, the popular anti-system despair, which the Nazis remorselessly exploited, would have ebbed away (Holtfrerich, 1990a, pp. 72–4). The decline of the Nazi vote in the second (November) Reichstag election of 1932, coinciding as it did with the first non-seasonal decline in unemployment since the slump began, seemed to show the crisis-sensitivity of the Nazi vote.

The third point aroused a lively debate on the views of politicians, civil servants, trade unionists and the general public. A central figure in this debate is Hans Schäffer. The tenor of his above-mentioned 'position paper' of September 1931 is remarkably at odds with the official advice he was tendering about raising taxes and controlling expenditure. Because he considered the 1932–3 budget irresponsibly risky he resigned his post on 2 May 1932 (James, 1986, pp. 338f; Patch, 1998, pp. 201–4, 217f, 256f). But in any case, a simple poll of participants' fiscal views may miss the point. It is easy to conceive of multiparty interactions where each party's starting position is a commitment to budgetary balance but, because expenditure proposals are less unpopular than tax proposals, each party compromises more readily on the latter than the former, thus in the end agreeing a deficit budget. The weak German party system, where the left was as intransigently opposed to higher indirect taxation as the right to higher direct taxation, agreed to budgetary balance from the turn of the century to 1945 only in 1923–4 and 1930–2, when parliamentary control was circumvented by Enabling Law or Emergency Decree. And in fact, from 1929, the political consensus supported tax cuts (albeit predicated upon a balanced budget). Hilferding, the SPD Finance Minister, had heeded the strident complaints of business regarding over-taxation in the Weimar welfare- and reparations-state, and agreed to devote the 'Young Plan' reduction of the reparations annuity to tax cuts. His intention had been frustrated by the outcome of the December fiscal crisis, (see also below) when he and his State Secretary had resigned. But Brüning came to power committed to the same tax-cutting policy in the medium (though not the short) term (Meister, 1991, p. 171).

Borchardt's fourth point has received the most attention in the recent debate. James (1986, pp.53–73; 1990, p. 44), followed by Balderston (1993), Bachmann's detailed monograph (1996), and Ritschl (1998), argued that the real reason why taxes were raised and expenditure cut was because deficits could not be financed and the alternative was State bankruptcy. People accustomed to well-oiled Anglo-Saxon fiscal machines (the last time the British State even partly defaulted on its debts was 1672) can hardly imagine a government constantly faced with the prospect of being unable to pay civil service salaries at the end of the month or make the agreed transfers of tax revenues to the federal states. Yet this was the re-peated situation of the German Reich from 1929 to 1932. The reason was its inability to borrow. From spring 1929 to Christmas the 'great coalition' under Herman Müller had been plagued by this problem. Only 183m reichsmark of its 300m reichsmark domestic loan of May 1929 (500m reichsmarks had been originally planned) was subscribed, a good deal of that by public bodies, and this despite the bait of tax exemption on the interest for private subscribers. For the rest of the year the government relied on a succession of foreign credits, the last of which in December 1929 attracted the united opposition of the Agent-General for Reparations and Reichsbank President Schacht. The former feared that haphazard foreign bor-rowing by the Reich might spoil the market for the Reparations ('Young') Loan planned for 1930.

Short-term borrowing from the banks proved equally difficult, particularly after the first run on bank deposits during the reparations crisis of April–May 1929. The eventual solution to the December 1929 crisis was a credit from a bank consortium, which really amounted to a covert Reichsbank credit (Bachmann, 1996, pp. 127–78). Short-term borrowing from the banks again became very sticky from autumn 1930 with the resurgent banking crisis, and became impossible thereafter.

The fiscal embarrassment of the Reich had made it desperate for any immediate reparations relief and so weakened its bargaining power with the Allies over the Young Plan. Brüning came to office determined to ensure by fiscal reforms that this never happened again. But, as Bachmann (1996) demonstrates, the timing of his expenditure cuts and tax increases was driven not by his principles but the recurrence of cash-flow crises threatening to bankrupt the Reich. His emergency measures tended to be barely adequate, particularly over the winter of 1932, and, as stated above, this minimalism precipitated the resignation of Hans Schäffer.

Clingan (2001, pp. 118, 164, 183f) argued that if the Reich had nurtured a market for treasury bills in the mid-1920s, and if Brüning had worked with the SPD in the slump, avoiding the 1930 election and resort to 'Emergency Decrees', the tourniquet constricting its spending could have been progressively eased. However, if neither bond markets nor banks at home nor abroad would lend, why did the government not monetise the debt? In fact it did: a sign of the government's desperation was the large amounts of new coinage that were minted and used to meet government bills in 1931–2, the government profiting from the seignorage. But to monetise its debt on a large scale would have needed the creation of money balances at the Reichsbank, which would have required the Reichsbank to circumvent the statutory limitations on its lending to the Reich. This did happen on a large scale during the Third Reich and the techniques were already used on a small scale under Brüning. Was the real cause of the cash problems of the Reich the obstinacy of Hans Luther, the Reichsbank President? (Tilly and Huck, 1994, pp. 91f; Patch, 1998, pp. 87f, 209f, 261)

Ritschl and Balderston argue in different ways that the Reichsbank had no room for manoeuvre either. Ritschl's (1998) argument implies that if the Reichsbank had monetised government debt, in the short run this would create money balances in excess of the demand for them, some of which the balance-holders would attempt to convert into foreign currencies. But if the Young Plan had made foreigners unwilling to lend to Germany, these attempts would exhaust Germany's foreign reserves and force her off the gold standard. This would alienate the USA, on whose goodwill Brüning counted for agreed reparations annulment and for the revival of foreign lending after the end of reparations which he viewed as vital to German economic recovery. *Ex post*, this strategy proved pointless, for with US unwillingness to lend in the 1930s because of defaults on every hand and trade restrictions preventing export-led recovery, Germany might as well have unilaterally terminated reparations payments. What happened, vindicated the Nazis. *Ex ante*, however, Brüning's policies were unimpeachable. Most defences of a Keynesian reflationary alternative presume, wrongly (in Ritschl's eyes), the possibility of foreign borrowing.

Balderston (1993, pp. 266–331) argued that the financial markets drew a connection between the indiscipline of German fiscal politics and the gold standard regime, which severely limited the Reichsbank's freedom of action. He distinguished between the kind of controlled deficit that Keynesian economists envisage, presupposing British-style governments fully in control of their budgets and the kind of uncontrolled, unpredictable deficit that the fragile German multiparty coalitions – including Brüning's weak minority cabinet – could be forced into if the financing were available. German history, particularly (but not solely) since 1918 was replete with examples of the kind of fiscal irresponsibility on which the weak German coalitions usually composed their internal political differences. The clamour for tax-reduction in 1929–30 underlined the difficulty of securing budgetary balance in the recession. His argument was that since future budget surpluses that could limit the rise of public debts were judged unlikely, given the party-political constellation, the markets would not lend and that the actual deficits therefore placed the Reichsbank in a 'double bind'. If it financed the deficit, it re-established the inflation period monetary regime and the markets might drive Germany off the gold standard. If it did not finance the deficit, this might force a Reich bankruptcy with incalculable consequences for the banks and the German financial system. Thus the deficitary dynamic in the Reich's finances made the currency markets exceedingly nervous of the reichsmark. This made accommodatory action by the Reichsbank next to impossible (the argument presupposes that with a free press any covert breach of these limitations would quickly have been spotted by the financial journalists). The emphasis often placed on the possibilities of French loans being squandered by an obstinate anti-French foreign policy (Ferguson and Temin, 2001) overlooks the difficulty of persuading the French market in those years to make any substantial foreign loans.

Balderston argued that the threat of Reich bankruptcy was what ultimately gave Brüning the power to keep the parties 'on side' *on his own terms* in this period. This threat would not explain the relatively tame acceptance of the price-, wage- and interest-rate-cutting measures in the Fourth Emergency Decree of December 1931, however. The more friction-free route to the same end would have been devaluation, following Britain off the gold standard. Devaluation by such a hugely indebted country might have triggered a destabilising depreciation, (cf., on the recent Asian crises, Corbett and Vines, 1999). It would have worsened the insolvency of the thinly capitalised great banks with their large foreign currency deposits, by increasing the non-performance of the foreign-currency-denominated loans in which form they had lent on the deposits, and threatened the conclusion of the standstill agreements. But this does not explain why the solution of capital controls plus devaluation was not pursued, as this would at least have stemmed the export slide (but see Borchardt, 1984).

Why then did the Nazi reflation (without devaluation) succeed? Ritschl emphasised the end of reparations. Balderston argued that the replacement of the multiparty by the one-party State made the deficits seem more controlled and thus encouraged an – albeit reticent – revival of domestic lending to the State. Clingan (2001, p. 212) argued that the Nazi reflation could already have been implemented by Brüning in 1930 if he had had the wit.

No consensus on the reasons for the Brüning deflation is in sight. In part this is because the arguments rest on suppositions about how the markets would have reacted to counterfactual alternative policies – and these are hard to prove.

**The end of the slump**

Registered unemployment stopped rising in May 1932. Deseasonalised, it was 0.5m lower at the end of the year than in the middle. The employment stimulation measures of the von Papen regime have been credited with this effect, as has the ending of reparations at the Lausanne Conference of June 1932. Von Papen's measures centred on an ingenious scheme to pay contractors on certain public works projects with certificates that could be used between 1934 and 1938 to extinguish tax liabilities. These could be sold immediately for cash to investors. This scheme was also to be used to reward employers hiring extra workers and was connected to a (short-lived) empowerment to reduce the rates of pay on the 31st to the 40th hours worked by the additional workers. The total expenditure contemplated was 1.5bn reichsmarks – quite large in fiscal terms. Von Papen's public works scheme was reinforced by the 500m reichsmarks 'Immediate Programme' of the short-lived von Schleicher government, announced on January 28 1933, two days before it was replaced by the Hitler–von Papen–Hugenberg government (Guillebaud, 1939).

The efficacy of von Papen's measures would depend on the credibility of his regime, and as in September 1932 it suffered the worst no-confidence defeat in German history, this cannot have been high. So the ending of reparations remains a better candidate for causing the end of the slump. But it rests on the presumption that until June 1932 the markets had still been betting on Germany having to pay substantial amounts. A final possibility is the natural self-reviving properties of a capitalist economy (James,1993). The end to destocking by business, because nothing more could be destocked, could have played an important part in the early stages.

# 6
# Epilogue

This short book has studied how Germany's external and internal political uncertainties may have interacted with the decisions of savers, spenders, borrowers, lenders, job-offerers and job-seekers in shaping the tumultuous economic history of the Weimar Republic. It did not have the space to explore how the same interactions may have shaped the Republic's political history and ultimate collapse. Much emphasis was placed upon international interactions: especially between reparations and currency collapse, currency collapse and the Dawes Plan, the Dawes Plan and foreign lending, the Young Plan, or challenges to it, and the cessation of foreign lending.

Emphasis was also placed on domestic interactions: between Germany's internecine domestic conflicts (fought out over the budget and in the arena of labour relations) and monetary history and economic growth. Budgetary conflict was either resolved via monetary expansion (as during the inflation) or threatened to contradict the monetary regime (as after 1924), with possible repercussions for the financial crisis. Business and labour fought a bitter trench warfare as the former sought to retake and the latter to defend, the salient captured through the revolutionary social policy and the 'Stinnes–Legien' agreement. Unlike the Western Front, this conflict had an umpire – the State, which feared that the defeat of either side could imperil the Republic. As a result, as little ground changed hands as in any First World War offensive. Borchardt argued persuasively that the stalemate squeezed profits and prevented the investment and growth needed for permanently resolving the conflict.

Germany's conflicts, both external and internal, were fanned by global political uncertainty. No effective successor was devised in the 1920s to the 'Concert of Great Powers' in Europe, which for a century before it failed in 1914, had prevented local conflicts from spreading. Without active US engagement and with the weakening of western European powers by the war and of eastern Europe by territorial balkanisation, Germany remained potentially the greatest continental power, able to exploit conflicts of economic and diplomatic interest between France and the Anglo-Saxons. These changes created the scope both for the reparations conflict abroad and for Germans at home to indulge in their internecine domestic conflicts; and they encouraged ambitions on the German right.

However, real history can never be neatly squeezed into any analytical framework. Politics and economics may have been less interconnected than this book has suggested. German 'catch-up' on the US economy may have been impeded by an apolitical sclerosis of the German entrepreneurial system (James, 1986) or temporary technical difficulties in adopting 'Fordism'. The depositors who toppled the German banks in 1931 may have simply been punishing the bad business judgements of the bankers. Rising wages and low profits after 1924 may just have reflected market conditions. The alternation of *global* slump and recovery in this era stood in no clear relation to global politics. Maybe Brüning's hands were tied by nothing more than his own character and political ineptitude (Clingan, 2001). Moreover, the insights of economic theory should not be overrated. Economic theory is the attempt to imagine rational relations between data in relation to what *has* taken place. The imagination is always influenced by the knowledge of what happened later – and by the prevailing economic 'paradigm'. We forget the infinity of other unimagined rational relations that could 'explain' the data, let alone temporary irrational derangements. Neither the simple economics used here, nor any logically superior macroeconomics of present or future, can leap the chasm that divides us from the minds of the historical actors. The true reasons for what they did will only be revealed on the day when God judges the secrets of men's hearts (Romans 2:16). The sombre connection of the history studied in this book and the Nazi catastrophe should make the historian ready to doubt what he thinks he knows.

# Glossary of economic and
political terms

**Annuity:** Here used to mean an annual payment of reparations due to the Allies.

**Asset(s):** Any durable possession which yields an economic benefit and/or can be sold for money.

**Balance of current transactions:** This is the balance between exports and imports of goods and services, visible and invisible, and is thus one element of the balance of payments.

**Balance of payments:** The balance between a country's receipts of and payments of foreign currency. Thus exports of goods and services earn foreign currency and are a plus, imports of the same a minus; capital lending to abroad (or repayments of previous capital borrowing from abroad) a minus, capital borrowing from abroad (or, foreign repayment of previous lending to abroad) a plus. Where the sum of these is positive the balance of payments is in surplus, where negative, in deficit.

**'Base money':** See **monetary base**.

**Bill(s):** Or 'bill(s) of exchange'. An undertaking by the drawee to pay a fixed sum at a future date. A bill bears no interest, hence sells in advance of the due date at a discount. Bills on private drawees are called 'trade' or 'commercial' bills; on the state, 'treasury' bills. See Discounting and Discount rate.

**Budget deficit(s):** The budget is the sum of all government expenditure and income. In this book it refers to Reich expenditure and income. A budget deficit arises when government spending is greater than government current income, defined as tax revenues plus the (in the German case considerable) state income from its enterprises and properties. A government must borrow to finance the excess spending when it runs a deficit.

**Budget surplus/surpluses:** A budget surplus arises when government spending is less than government current income, defined as tax revenues plus state income from state-run enterprises and properties. A government will usually repay debt when it runs a surplus.

**Capital import:** Capital borrowed from abroad.

**Capital market:** The market on which financial securities are traded.

**Cartel(s):** Usually a time-limited agreement among independent producers to limit competition amongst themselves in various ways. Some cartels of the Weimar Republic were compulsory and permanent.

**Centre Party:** The Catholic Party (though not all Catholics voted for it). It had a remarkably irreducible constituency throughout the lifetime of the Republic.

**Collective labour contracts:** Fixed-term agreements between employers' associations and trades unions covering wages and other working conditions. These were supported by the Weimar State and the unions but contested by many employers.

**Cyclical:** Pertaining to changes in aggregate demand for all goods and services, as opposed to particular demand for specific goods and services.

**DDP:** The German Democratic Party – the more left-leaning of the Weimar Republic's two liberal parties. After early success in 1919 it suffered progressive erosion of voter support, especially from the young. For the September 1930 Reichstag election it concluded a shotgun (and short-lived) marriage with the 'Order of Young Germans' and was renamed 'The German State Party'. See **DVP**.

**Discounting:** The selling of a trade or treasury bill, often to the central bank, at a discount, in advance of its repayment date. The difference between the purchase price and the repayment price of a trade or treasury bill, expressed as a percentage of the repayment price, is the discount rate.

**Discount rate:** See **Discounting**.

**DNVP:** The German National People's Party. This was the conservative party, and had landowner and business support. It moved from a rigid anti-republican stance to occasional participation in government in the mid-1920s before moving back to a rigid oppositional stance under Hugenberg in the early 1930s.

**DVP:** The German People's Party – the more right-leaning of the Weimar Republic's two liberal parties. After a shaky start in 1919 it attracted more votes than the DDP. It had significant business support. But its support also fell heavily from 1930. Its famous leader up to his death in 1929 was Stresemann.

**Fiscal:** Pertaining to government spending and taxing policy (including, in the German case, other earned income, especially from the railroads to 1924).

**Forward exchange rate of the mark:** The price in sterling agreed now for undertaking to deliver marks at some future date – say one month's or three months' time – and to be paid at time of delivery. The 'spot' rate is the price in sterling paid now for marks delivered immediately. If the 'forward' price exceeds the 'spot' this implies that the mark exchange rate against sterling is expected to be higher in the future than at the present.

**Goldmark:** A unit of account during the inflation defined as a dollar multiplied by 4.2 – the prewar mark–dollar exchange rate.

**Gold standard:** A monetary system based on the commitment of the central bank to sell/buy gold at fixed prices in the national currency. If more than one country's central bank makes this commitment, the exchange rates between their currencies will fluctuate only within narrow limits.

**Human capital:** The value of the occupationally relevant training and skills of a worker.

**Hyperinflation:** Conventionally defined as a rate of price increase exceeding 50% per month.

**Insolvent:** The condition where the debts of an individual or firm exceed their assets.

**Investment:** Normally used by economists to denote construction or acquisition of real capital – e.g. buildings, machinery, stocks of materials that can be employed in the production process. In the phrase, 'foreign investment', however, it denotes acquisition of financial assets.

**Investment ratio:** Investment spending as a ratio of national income.

**Invisible:** Pertaining to exports and imports of intangible services – e.g. banking, shipping, tourism; interest income and repatriated profits on foreign investment.

**Kaiserreich:** The German state from 1871 to 1918.

**KPD:** The German Communist Party, founded at the end of 1918, greatly enlarged following the dissolution of the USPD. See **USPD**.

**Liquidity:** Possession of cash; or of assets, which can quickly be sold for a predeterminable amount of cash.

**Mark-denominated asset(s):** A financial asset whose value is contracted in mark currency. See **Asset(s)**.

**Maturity:** The date at which a debt (e.g. a bill or bond) is due for repayment.

**'Mobilising':** In connection with reparations this refers to the marketing of bonds whose interest and repayment are to be met out of German reparations payments. Thus the French hoped to obtain immediately, via an 'advance' from the world's capital markets, what the Germans were due to pay over many years.

**Monetisation:** The financing of a budget deficit by increasing the money supply.

**Monetary base:** Reichsbank notes plus deposits in accounts at the Reichsbank.

**Money:** In this book, 'money' is defined as 'what is acceptable as payment'.

**Money balances:** The stock of money possessed by an individual, firm or other institution.

**Money demand:** The demand for money balances to hold as an asset.

**Money supply:** The stock of money balances held in pockets or in bank accounts by all individuals, firms, and levels of government other than the Reich.

**MSPD:** The 'Majority Social Democratic Party' of Germany – the larger wing of the SPD which in 1917 continued to support the war effort. See **USPD**.

**National income:** The sum of all personal incomes in a country.

**Nominal:** Means 'in money terms', and is used by economists in contrast to 'real'. If I lend £100 for one year at 5% interest, I get back, in total, £105. But if prices have risen 5% in the year, that £105 is worth £100 at start-of-period prices, and the real rate of interest is 0%. It can be seen then, that during inflations, 'real' interest rates are below 'nominal'.

**Non-tradables:** See **Tradables**.

**Participation rate:** The number of people in or seeking work as a proportion of the same age-group in the population.

**Policy regime:** A set of principles guiding the conduct of economic policy and enabling the markets to predict how policy will change as economic circumstances change.

**Primary products:** Agricultural goods and other (e.g. mined) raw materials.

**Real:** Denotes a monetary quantity deflated to eliminate the effect of price change. Thus a rising 'real' income means that money incomes had risen faster than/fallen less fast than prices.

**Real exchange rate:** This is the level of a country's prices, converted into foreign currency at the current rate, and compared with foreign prices. If it rises, German prices, so converted, rise relative to foreign prices.

**Reich:** Used to denote German central (or, federal) government.

**Reichsbank:** The German central bank.

**Reichsmark:** The new German gold-standard currency from 1924.

**Reichstag:** The German national (or federal) parliament.

**Rent:** In addition to its normal sense, used to denote the excess profit derived from some market advantage.

**Seignorage:** The difference between the cost of production and the face value of a coinage or note issue, which can be appropriated as profit by the issuer.

**Socialisation:** Taking into 'social' or 'national' ownership.

**SPD:** The Social Democratic Party of Germany; after about 1922 the 'democratic socialist' party, in contrast to the KPD.

**Supervisory Board(s):** German company law requires public limited companies to have a management board plus a supervisory board on which sat the representatives of the shareholders and creditors, notably the bank with which the firm mainly deals.

**Terms of trade:** Export prices expressed as a ratio of import prices. If the terms of trade improve (i.e. rise) Germany can buy a larger quantum of imports by the sale of a given quantum of exports. This increases German 'real' incomes.

**Tradables:** Goods and services that can be sold to or bought from abroad, and thus are subject to foreign competition. Non-tradables (e.g. haircuts) are not so subject.

**Trade balance:** See **Balance of current transactions**.

**Trade bills:** See **Bill(s)**.

**Trade deficit:** See **Balance of current transactions**.

**Trade surplus:** See **Balance of current transactions**.

**Trade unions:** German trade unions before the 1940s divided into three ideologically distinguished groupings. Of the 3m or so trade unionists in 1913, about $2\frac{1}{2}$m were members of 'Free', or Socialist unions, about 350,000 of 'Christian' (Catholic) unions and the remainder, mainly skilled engineers, of 'Hirsch-Duncker' or liberal unions. The importance of the Christian unions rested on their significant membership in the Ruhr coal mines.

**Transfer:** Here used to denote the acquisition of foreign currencies in which to make cash reparations payments to the Allies.

**Treasury bills:** See **Bills**.

**USPD:** The Independent Social Democratic Party of Germany – the group which seceded from the SPD in 1917, refusing to continue to vote for parliamentary sanction for government war borrowing. Opposition to the war was what held it together, and it dissolved itself in 1923, its members either joining the KPD or the MSPD, which renamed itself the SPD.

**Visible:** Pertaining to exports and imports of tangible goods.

# Bibliography

Abelshauser, W. (1978) Inflation und Stabilisierung. Zum Problem ihrer makroökonomischen Auswirkungen auf die Rekonstruktion der deutschen Wirtschaft nach dem Ersten Weltkrieg. In Büsch, O. and Feldman, G. D. (eds.) *Historische Prozesse der deutschen Inflation 1914–1924. Ein Tagungsbericht.* pp. 161–74. Berlin. This work and the next expound a view of Weimar economic history as a postwar reconstruction which inflation facilitated but stabilisation interrupted.

Abelshauser, W. and Petzina, D. (1981) Krise und Rekonstruktion. Zur Interpretation der gesamtwirtschaftlichen Entwicklung im 20. Jahrhundert. Reprinted in Abelshauser, W. and Petzina, D. (eds.) *Deutsche Wirtschaftsgeschichte im Industriezeitalter,* Königstein/Ts: 47–93.

Ambrosius, L. E. (1987) *Woodrow Wilson and the American Diplomatic Tradition. The Treaty Fight in Perspective.* Cambridge.

Angell, J. W. (1926) *The Theory of International Payments.* Cambridge, MA. (1929) *The Economic Recovery of Germany.* New Haven, CT. A classic contemporary economic analysis, ending with a mistaken optimism!

Bachmann, U. (1996) *Reichskasse und öffentlicher Kredit in der Weimarer Republik 1924–1932.* Frankfurt. Thorough, source-based analysis of the fiscal problem of the Reich.

Balderston, T. (1983) The beginning of the depression in Germany: investment and the capital market. *Economic History Review,* 36, 395–415.

(1985) Links between inflation and depression. In Feldman, G. D. (ed.) *Die Nachwirkungen der Inflation auf die deutsche Geschichte 1924 bis 1933.* pp. 157–185. Munich.

(1991) German banking between the wars: the crisis of the credit banks. *Business History Review,* 65, 554–605.

(1993) *The Origins and Course of the German Economic Crisis. November 1923 to May 1932.* Berlin.

(1995a) A strong German economy: a precondition for the revitalization of the European market? In Petricioli, M. (ed.) *A Missed Opportunity? 1922: The Reconstruction of Europe.* Bern.

(1995b) German and British monetary policy, 1919–1932. In Feinstein, C. H. (ed.) *Banking, Currency and Finance in Europe between the Wars.* pp. 151–86. Oxford.

Barclay, D. E. (1986) The insider as outsider: Rudolf Wissell's critique of Social Democratic economic policies, 1919–1920. In Feldman, G. D., Holtfrerich, C.-L., Ritter, G. A., Witt, P. C. (eds.) *The Adaptation to Inflation.* pp. 451–71. Berlin.

Barkai, A. (1990) *Nazi Economics: Ideology, Theory and Policy.* Oxford [German original, 1977].

Bessel, R. (1993) *Germany after the First World War.* Oxford. Excellent study of demobilisation at the 'grass roots'.

Bergmann, C. (1927) *The History of Reparations.* London.

Borchardt, K. (1984) Could and should Germany have followed Great Britain in leaving the gold standard? *Journal of European Economic History,* 13, 471–97.

(1990) A decade of debate about Brüning's economic policies. In Kruedener, J. Freiherr von (ed.) *Economic Crisis and Political Collapse: The Weimar Republic 1924–1933.* pp 99–151. New York.

(1991) Constraints and room for manoeuvre in the great depression of the early thirties: towards a revision of the received historical picture. In Borchardt, K. *Perspectives on Modern German Economic History and Policy.* Cambridge [German original, 1979].

Borchardt, K. and Schötz, H.-O. (eds.) (1991) *Wirtschaftspolitik in der Krise. Die (Geheim)-Konferenz der Friedrich-List-Gesellschaft im September 1931 über Möglichkeiten und Folgen einer Kreditausweitung.* Baden-Baden. A transcription of the discussions at a critical conference on reflation held in September 1931.

Born, K. E. (1983) *International Banking in the Nineteenth and Twentieth Centuries.* Leamington Spa.

Brady, R. A. (1933) *The Rationalisation Movement in German Industry: A Study in the Evolution of Economic Planning.* Berkeley. A major study by a US sociologist.

Braun, H.-J. (1990) *The German Economy in the Twentieth Century.* London.

Bresciani-Turroni, C. (1937) *The Economics of Inflation. A Study of Currency Depreciation in Post-war Germany, 1914–1923.* London [Italian original, 1931]. The classic 'quantity theory' text.

Broadberry, S. N. and Ritschl, A. (1994) The iron twenties: real wages, productivity and the lack of prosperity in Britain and Germany before the Great Depression. In Buchheim, C., Hutter, M., James, H. (eds.) *Zerrissene Zwischenkriegszeit. Wirtschaftshistorische Beiträge. Knut Borchardt zum 65 Geburtstag.* pp. 15–44. Baden-Baden.

Broadberry, S. N. and Wagner, K. (1996) Human capital and productivity in manufacturing during the twentieth century: Britain, Germany and the United States. In Ark, B. van and Crafts, N. (eds.) *Quantitative Aspects of Post-War European Economic Growth.* pp. 244–70. Cambridge.

Brown, B. (1988) *Monetary Chaos in Europe. The End of an Era.* London.

Burdekin, R. C. K. and Burkett, P. (1992) Money, credit and wages in hyperinflation: post-World-War I Germany. *Economic Inquiry* 30, 479–95. Reprinted in Siklos, P. (ed.) *Great Inflations of the 20th Century: Theories, Policies and Evidence.* pp. 185–207. Aldershot. A recent defence of the importance of wage pressure in the inflation.

Burnett, P. M. (1940) *Reparation at the Paris Peace Conference from the Standpoint of the American Delegation.* Abridged edition. New York.

Cagan, P. (1956) The monetary dynamics of hyperinflation. In Friedman, M. (ed.) *Studies in the Quantity Theory of Money.* pp. 25–117. Chicago. Classic study of the demand for money in hyperinflation.

Cantwell, J. (1995) The evolution of European industrial technology in the interwar period. In Caron, F., Erkner, P., Fischer, W. (eds.) *Innovations in the European Economy between the Wars.* pp. 277–309. Berlin.

Carsten, F. L. (1972) *Revolution in Central Europe 1918–1919.* London. Classic study.

Clingan, C. E. (2001) *Finance from Kaiser to Führer. Budget Politics in Germany 1912–1934.* Westport, CT. Strongly argues Brüning's culpability.

Cohn, R. L. (1997) Fiscal policy in Germany during the Great Depression. In Komlos, J. and Eddie, S. (eds.) *Selected Cliometric Studies on German History.* pp. 261–83. Stuttgart. Calculates Germany's 'full-employment fiscal balance' in the slump.

Corbett, D. (1994) Wage woes in Weimar: a partial investigation. In Grantham, G. and Mackinnon, M. (eds.) *Labour Market Evolution. The Economic History of Market Integration, Wage Flexibility and the Employment Relation.* pp. 225–44. London.

Corbett, J. and Vines, D. (1999) The Asian crisis: lessons from the collapse of financial systems, exchange rates and macroeconomic policy. In Agenor, P.-R., Miller, M., Vines, D., Weber, A. (eds.) *The Asian Financial Crisis. Causes, Contagion and Consequences.* pp. 67–110. Cambridge.

Costigliola, F. (1984) *Awkward Dominion. American Political, Economic, and Cultural Relations with Europe, 1919–1933.* Ithaca, NY. Important study of the economic aspects of US policy towards Europe.

Dornbusch, R. (1987) Lessons from the German inflation experience of the 1920s. In Dornbusch, R., Fischer, S., Bosson, J. (eds.) *Macroeconomics and Finance. Essays in Honor of Franco Modigliani.* pp. 337–66. Cambridge, MA.

Dornseifer, B. (1995) Strategy, technological capability and innovation: German enterprises in comparative perspective. In Caron, F.,

Erkner, P., Fisher, W. (eds.) *Innovations in the European Economy between the wars*. pp.197–226. Berlin.

Einzig, P. (1937) *The Theory of Forward Exchange*. London. Definitions, analysis, statistics.

Ellis, H. S. (1937) *German Monetary Theory 1905–1933*. Cambridge, MA. Contemporary expositions of the 'quantity' and 'balance of payments' theories of the inflation.

Evans, R. and Geary, D. (eds.) (1987) *The German Unemployed*. London.

Feldenkirchen, W. (1987) Big business in interwar Germany: organizational innovation at Vereinigte Stahlwerke, I.G. Farben and Siemens. *Business History Review*, 61, 417–51. Major analysis of their management structures.

(1999) *Siemens 1918–1945*. Columbus, OH [German original, 1995].

Feldman, G. D. (1966) *Army, Industry and Labor in Germany 1914–1918*. Princeton. Classic analysis of the German political economy of the First World War.

(1970) German business between war and inflation. The origins of the Stinnes–Legien Agreement. In Ritter, Gerhard A. (ed.) *Entstehung und Wandel der modernen Gesellschaft. Festschrift für Hans Rosenberg*. Berlin. A classic analysis, emphasising the agreement's pre-revolutionary roots.

(1975) Economic and social problems of the German demobilization 1918–1919. *Journal of Modern History*, 47, 1–47. Emphasises the 'demobilisation' perspective on the German political economy of the Armistice.

(1977) *Iron and Steel in the German Inflation 1916–1923*. Princeton.

(1982) The political economy of Germany's relative stabilization during the 1920–21 depression. In Feldman, G. D., Holtfrerich, C.-L., Ritter, G. A., Witt, P. C. (eds.) *The German Inflation Reconsidered. A Preliminary Balance*. pp. 180–206. Berlin. Major study, emphasising domestic political dynamics.

(1993) *The Great Disorder: Politics, Economics and Society in the German Inflation 1914–1924*. New York. His *magnum opus* on the inflation arguing its socially destructive effects.

(1995) The Deutsche Bank from world war to world economic crisis. In Gall, L., Feldman, G. D., James, H., Holtfrerich, C.-L., Büschgen, H. E. *The Deutsche Bank 1870–1995*. London.

(1998) A comment. In Boemecke, M. F., Feldman, G. D., Glaser, E. (eds.) *The Treaty of Versailles. A Reassessment after 75 Years*. pp. 441–47. Cambridge.

Felix, D. (1971a) Reparations reconsidered with a vengeance. *Central European History*, 4, 171–9. Important 'Germanophile' article.

(1971b) *Walther Rathenau and the Weimar Republic. The Politics of Reparations.* Baltimore.

Ferguson, N. (1995) *Paper and Iron. Hamburg Business and German Politics in the Era of Inflation 1897–1927.* Cambridge.

(1996) Constraints and room for manoeuvre in the German inflation of the early 1920s. *Economic History Review* 49, 435–66. Important thesis on costs/benefits of the inflation.

(1997) The German interwar economy: political choice versus economic determinism. In Fulbrook, M. (ed.) *German History since 1800.* London.

(1998) The balance of payments question: Versailles and after. In Boemecke, M. F., Feldman, G. D., Glaser, E. (eds.) *The Treaty of Versailles. A Reassessment after 75 Years.* pp. 401–40. Cambridge.

Ferguson, T. and Temin, P. (2001) Made in Germany: the German currency crisis of July 1931. Unpublished paper: JEL No. N14, E32.

Fergusson, A. (1975) *When Money Dies. The Nightmare of Weimar Collapse.* London.

Franco, G. H. B. (1990) Fiscal reforms and stabilisation: four hyperinflation cases examined. *Economic Journal* 100, 176–87.

Frenkel, J. A. (1979) Further evidence on expectations and the demand for money during the German hyperinflation. *Journal of Monetary Economics*, 5, 97–104.

(1982) Comment. In Kindleberger, C. P. and Laffargue, J.-P. (eds.) *Financial Crises: Theory, History and Policy.* pp.136–143. Cambridge.

Freyberg, T. von (1989) *Industrielle Rationalisierung in der Weimarer Republik. Untersucht an Beispielen aus dem Maschinenbau und der Elektroindustrie.* Frankfurt. Excellent study of 'Fordism' in engineering.

Führer, K. C. (1990) *Arbeitslosigkeit und die Entstehung der Arbeitslosenversicherung in Deutschland 1902–1927.* Berlin. Study of origins of unemployment insurance.

Graham, F. D. (1925) Germany's capacity to pay and reparations plan. *American Economic Review*, XV, 209–27. Neoclassical critique of the 'structuralist' arguments against reparations.

(1930) *Exchange, Prices and Production in Hyper-Inflation Germany 1920–1923.* Princeton. Classic study of the inflation, (cautiously) arguing its benefits.

Gregor, N. (1998) *Daimler–Benz in the Third Reich.* New Haven, CT. An illuminating business history, with pre-1933 section.

Guillebaud, C. W. (1939) *The Economic Recovery in Germany from 1933 to the Incorporation of Austria in March 1938.* London.

Guttmann, W. and Meehan, P. (1975) *The Great Inflation. Germany 1919–1923.* Westmead.

Hardach, G. (1970) Reichsbankpolitik und wirtschaftliche Entwicklung
1924–31. *Schmollers Jahrbuch*, 90/2, 563–92. A good Keynesian analysis of the deflationary effects of the post-stabilization gold standard.
(1976) *Weltmarktorientierung und relative Stagnation in Deutschland.
Währungspolitik in Deutschland 1924–31*. Berlin. A fine political-
monetary history.
Hayes, P. (1987) *Industry and Ideology. I.G. Farben in the Nazi Era*.
Cambridge. A groundbreaking business history, including chapters
on the pre-1933 period.
Helbich, W. J. (1962) *Reparationen in der Ära Brüning. Zur Bedeutung des
Young-Plans für die deutsche Politik*. Berlin. Argues the primacy of repa-
rations in Brüning's policies.
Helfferich, K. (1927) *Money*. London [translation of the sixth German
edition of 1923].
Hoffmann, W. G., Grumbach, F., Hesse, H. (1965) *Das Wachstum der
deutschen Wirtschaft seit der Mitte des 19. Jahrhunderts*. Berlin. The standard German historical national income calculations.
Holtfrerich, C.-L. (1983) Political factors of the German inflation. In
Schmukler, N. and Marcus, E. (eds.) *Inflation through the Ages: Economic, Social, Psychological and Historical Aspects*. pp. 400–16. New
York.
(1986) *The German Inflation 1914–1923. Causes and Effects in Interna-
tional Perspective*. Berlin [German original, 1980]. The major modern
economic-historical study.
(1990a) Economic policy options and the end of the Weimar Republic. In
Kershaw, I. (ed.) *Weimar: Why Did German Democracy Fail?* pp. 58–91.
London.
(1990b) Was the policy of deflation in Germany avoidable? In Kruedener,
J. Freiherr von (ed.) *Economic Crisis and Political Collapse: The Weimar
Republic 1924–1933*. pp. 63–80. New York.
Homburg, H. (1991) *Rationalisierung und Industriearbeit. Arbeitsmarkt –
Management – Arbeiterschaft im Siemens-Konzern Berlin 1900–1938*.
Berlin. Includes detailed study of 'Fordism' in electrical engineering.
Hubbard, W. (1990) The new inflation history. *Journal of Modern History*,
62, 552–69. Excellent literature survey.
Hughes, M. (1988) *Paying for the German Inflation*. Chapel Hill. Study of
the revaluation-of-debts controversy after the stabilisation.
Jacobson, J. 1989, The reparations settlement of 1924. In Feldman, G. D.,
Holtfrerich, C.-L., Ritter, G. A., Witt, P. C. (eds.) *The Consequences
of the Inflation*. pp. 79–108. Berlin.
James, H. (1984) The causes of the German banking crisis of 1931.
*Economic History Review*, 37, 68–87. A central study of the topic.
(1985) Did the Reichsbank draw the right lessons from the great inflation? In Feldman, G. D. (ed.) *Die Nachwirkungen der Inflation auf die
deutsche Geschichte 1924 bis 1933*. pp. 211–31. Munich.

(1986) *The German Slump. Politics and Economics 1924–1936.* Oxford. The standard work on Weimar politico-economic history after 1924.

(1990), Economic reasons for the collapse of Weimar. In Kershaw, I. (ed.) *Weimar: Why Did German Democracy Fail?* pp. 30–57. London.

(1993) Innovation and conservatism in economic recovery: the alleged Nazi recovery of the 1930s. In Garside, W. R. (ed.) *Capitalism in Crisis. International Responses to the Great Depression.* London.

Kent, B. (1989) *The Spoils of War: The Politics, Economics and Diplomacy of Reparations, 1918– 1932.* Oxford. The standard work on reparations.

Kershaw, I. (ed.) (1990) *Weimar: Why did German Democracy Fail?* London. Essays, mainly on the 'Borchardt' controversy.

Keylor, W. R. (1978) Rise and demise of the Franco-American Guarantee Pact, 1919-21. *Proceedings of the Annual Meeting of the Western Society for French History*, 15, 367–77.

Keynes, J. M. (1920) *The Economic Consequences of the Peace.* London: [first edition, 1919].

(1971) *The Revision of the Treaty.* Reprinted as *The Collected Writings of J. M. Keynes, Vol. III.* London. [first edition, 1922].

(1977) *Collected Writings. Vol. XVII. Activities 1920–22: treaty revision and reconstruction.* London.

Kindleberger, C. P. (1973) *The World in Depression 1929–1939.* London.

(1984a) A structural view of the German inflation. In Feldman, G. D., Holtfrerich, C.-L., Ritter, G. A., Witt, P. C. (eds.) *The Experience of Inflation. International and Comparative Studies.* pp. 10–33. Berlin. A central source for structural/distributional theories of the inflation.

(1984b) *A Financial History of Western Europe.* London.

Kocka, J. (1984) *Facing Total War. German Society 1914–1918.* Leamington Spa.

Kolb, E. (1988) *The Weimar Republic.* London [German original, 1984]. Excellent historiographic survey.

Kruedener, J. Freiherr von (1985) Die Überforderungen der Weimarer Republik als Sozialstaat. *Geschichte und Gesellschaft*, 11, 358–76. Argues that wages and welfare contributions overburdened the Weimar economy.

(ed.) (1990) *Economic Crisis and Political Collapse: The Weimar Republic 1924–1933.* New York. A collection of essays on the 'Borchardt' thesis.

Krüger, P. (1985) *Die Aussenpolitik der Republik von Weimar.* Darmstadt. A standard and illuminating diplomatic history.

Kunz, A. (1986) *Civil Servants and the Politics of Inflation in Germany 1914– 1924* Berlin.

Laursen, K. and Pedersen, J. (1964) *The German Inflation 1918–1923.* Amsterdam. A classic 'Keynesian' analysis centring on wage dynamics.

Leffler, M. P. (1979) *Elusive Quest: America's Pursuit of European Stability and French Security 1919–1933.* Chapel Hill. An illuminating study of the dynamics of US policy towards Europe.

Lentin. A. (1984) *Lloyd George, Woodrow Wilson, and the Guilt of Germany.* Leicester.

Lindenlaub, D. (1985) *Maschinenbauunternehmen in der deutschen Inflation 1919–1923.* Berlin. Challenges the view that inflation stimulated business investment.

Link, W. (1970) *Die amerikanische Stabilisierungspolitik in Deutschland, 1921–32.* Düsseldorf. Classic study of the political economy of US–German relations.

Liu, T.-L. (1999) *The Chameleon State. Global Culture and Policy Shifts in Britain and Germany 1914–1933.* New York.

Lyth, P. (1990) *Inflation and the Merchant Economy. The Hamburg Mittelstand 1914–1924.* New York. Excellent study of local impact of inflation.

Machlup, F. (1966) The transfer problem: theme and four variations. In Machlup, F. (ed.) *International Monetary Economics.* pp. 374–95. London.

Maier, C. S. (1975) *Recasting Bourgeois Europe: Stabilization Policy in France, Germany and Italy in the Decade after World War I.* Princeton. Ambitious study of post-1918 European political economy, arguing the innovation of 'corporatism' to restore social peace.

(1978) Die deutsche Inflation als Verteilungskonflikt: soziale Ursachen und Auswirkungen im internationalen Vergleich. In Büsch, O. and Feldman, G. D. (eds.) *Historische Prozesse der deutschen Inflation 1914–1924. Ein Tagungsbericht.* pp. 329–42. Berlin. A 'distributional' theory of the inflation.

(1984) Inflation and stabilization in the wake of two world wars: comparative strategies and sacrifices. In Feldman, G. D., Holtfrerich, C.-L., Ritter, G. A., Witt, P. C. (eds.) *The Experience of Inflation. International and Comparative Studies.* pp. 106–29. Berlin.

Marks, S. (1978) The myths of reparations. *Central European History*, 11, pp. 231–55. A classic 'Francophile' article.

(1998) Smoke and mirrors: in smoke-filled rooms and the Galerie des Glaces. In Boemecke, M. F., Feldman, G. D., Glaser, E. (eds.), *The Treaty of Versailles. A Reassessment after 75 Years.* pp. 337–70. Cambridge.

McDougal, W. A. (1978) *France's Rhineland Diplomacy, 1914–1924: The Last Bid for a Balance of Power in Europe.* Princeton. Important revisionist study of French reparations policy.

McNeil, W. C. (1986) *American Money and the Weimar Republic. Economics and Politics on the Eve of the Great Depression.* New York. An excellent politico-economic history.

Meakin, W. (1928) *The New Industrial Revolution. A Study for the General Reader of Rationalization and the Post-War Tendencies of Capitalism and Labour.* London.

Meister, R. (1991) *Die Grosse Depression: Zwangslagen und Handlungspielräume der Wirtschafts- und Finanzpolitik in Deutschland*

*1929–1932*. Regensburg. Important recent 'Keynesian' defence of the thesis of Brüning's culpability.

Michels, R. K. (1928) *Cartels, Combines and Trusts in Post-War Germany*. New York.

Mierzejewski, A. C. (1999) *The Most Valuable Asset of the Reich. A History of the German National Railway. Vol. 1: 1920–1932*. Chapel Hill, NC. A major business history.

Ministry of Labour (1931) *The Unemployment Problem in Germany. Translation of the Report of an Advisory Commission appointed by the Federal Government*. London.

Moeller, R. G. (1982) Winners as losers in the German inflation: peasant protest over the controlled economy. In Feldman, G. D., Holtfrerich, C.-L., Ritter, G. A., Witt, P. C. (eds.) *The German Inflation Reconsidered. A Preliminary Balance*. pp. 255–88. Berlin. Acute analysis of the role of state intervention in sparking protest.

Moulton, H. G. (1925) War debts and international trade theory. *American Economic Review*, XV, 700–16. The 'structural' case against reparations.

Moulton, H. G. and McGuire, C. E. (1923) *Germany's Capacity to Pay. A Study of the Reparation Problem*. New York. A classic statement of the 'structural' argument against reparations.

(1924) *The Reparation Plan. The Interpretation of the Reports of the Experts' Committees*. New York.

Niehuss, M. (1986) Lebensweise und Familie in der Inflationszeit. In Feldman, G. D., Holtfrerich, C.-L., Ritter, G. A., Witt, P. C. (eds.) *The Adaptation to Inflation*. pp. 237–65. Berlin. Major study of poverty in the inflation.

Nocken, U. (1974) Inter-industrial conflicts and alliances as exemplified by the AVI-Agreement. In Mommsen, H., Petzina, D., Weisbrod, B. (eds.) *Industrielles System und Politische Entwicklung in der Weimarer Republik*. Düsseldorf.

Nolan, M. (1994) *Visions of Modernity. American Business and the Modernization of Germany*. New York. A cultural history of rationalisation in the 1920s.

Northrop, M. B. (1938) *Control Policies of the Reichsbank*. New York. Good technical source.

Offer, A. (1989) *The First World War: An Agrarian Interpretation*. Oxford. Argues the critical leverage accorded by control of food and primary products.

Olson, M. (1982) *The Rise and Decline of Nations: Economic Growth, Stagflation and Social Rigidities*. Oxford.

Overy, R. J. (1996) *The Nazi Economic Recovery*. Cambridge [second edition, 1996].

Patch, W. L. Jr (1998) *Heinrich Brüning and the Dissolution of the Weimar Republic*. Cambridge. An indispensable political biography.

Petzina, D. (1969) Germany and the Great Depression. *Journal of Contemporary History*, 4/4, 59–71.

(1977) *Die deutsche Wirtschaft in der Zwischenkriegszeit*. Wiesbaden.

Plumpe, G. (1990) *Die I.G. Farbenindustrie AG: Wirtschaft, Technik und Politik 1904–1945*. Berlin. Detailed on technological and organisational history of I.G. Farben.

Preller, L. (1978; 1st edn 1949) *Sozialpolitik in der Weimarer Republik*. Düsseldorf. Classic history of Weimar social and labour policy by an ex-Labour Ministry official.

Pugh, M. (1993) *The Making of Modern British Politics 1867–1939*. Oxford.

Reckendrees, A. (2000) *Das Stahltrust-Projekt. Die Gründung der Vereinigten Stahlwerke A.G. und ihre Unternehmensentwicklung 1926–1933/4*. Munich. A major business history emphasising the 'short-termist' motives for the 1926 'steel trust'.

Ritschl, A. (1990) Zu hohe Löhne in der Weimarer Republik? Eine Auseinandersetzung mit Holtfrerichs Berechnungen zur Lohnposition der Arbeiterschaft 1925–1932. *Geschichte und Gesellschaft*, 16, 375–402. A major recalculation of the labour productivity data, vindicating Borchardt's view of the 'sick economy'.

(1998) Reparations transfers, the Borchardt hypothesis, and the Great Depression in Germany, 1929–32: a guided tour for hard-headed Keynesians. *European Review of Economic History*, 2, 49–72. Argues that the transition from the Dawes to the Young Plan precipitated a German foreign debt crisis and caused the severity of the German slump.

(in press) *Deutschlands Krise und Konjunktur. Binnenkonjunktur, Auslandsverschuldung und Reparationsproblem zwischen Dawes-Plan und Transfersperre 1924–1934*. Berlin.

Robinson, J. (1938) Review of *The Economics of Inflation* by C. Bresciani-Turroni. *Economic Journal*, 48, 507–13. An early statement of the 'wage' theory of the inflation.

Rowley, E. (1994) *Hyperinflation in Germany. Perceptions of a Process*. Aldershot. Informative on the man-in-the-street perception of hyperinflation.

Ryder, A. J. (1967) *The German Revolution of 1918. A Study of German Socialism in War and Revolt*. Cambridge.

Sanmann, H. (1965) Daten und Alternativen der deutschen Wirtschafts- und Finanzpolitik in der Ära Brüning. *Hamburger Jahrbuch für Wirtschafts- und Gesellschaftspolitik*, 10, 109–40. Classic political study of Brüning's policies on a 'Keynesian' view.

Sargent, T. J. (1982) The end of four big inflations. In Hall, R. (ed.) *Inflation: Causes and Effects*. pp. 41–97. Chicago.

Schmidt, C. T. (1934) *German Business Cycles 1924–1934*. New York.

Scholz, Robert (1986) Lohn und Beschäftigung als Indikatoren für die soziale Lage der Arbeiterschaft in der Inflation. In Feldman, G. D., Holtfrerich, C.-L., Ritter, G. A., Witt, P. C. (eds.) *The Adaptation to*

*Inflation.* pp. 278–322. Berlin. Challenges Holtfrerich's thesis of the relative benefits of inflation to workers.

Schubert, A. (1991) *The Credit-Anstalt Crisis of 1931.* Cambridge.

Schuker, S. (1988) *American 'Reparations' to Germany, 1919–1933: Implications for the Third-World Debt Crisis.* Princeton Studies in International Finance, No. 61. Princeton.

(1993) Origins of American stabilization policy in Europe: the financial dimension 1918–1924. In Schröder, H. J. (ed.) *Confrontation and Co-operation. Germany and the USA in the Era of World War I, 1900–1924.* Providence, RI.

(1998) The Rhineland question: west European security at the Paris Peace Conference of 1919. In Boemecke, M. F., Feldman, G. D., Glaser, E. (eds.) *The Treaty of Versailles. A Reassessment after 75 Years.* pp. 275–312. Cambridge.

Schumpeter, J. A. (1939) *Business Cycles. A Theoretical, Historical and Statistical Analysis of the Capitalist Process.* New York.

Sharp, Alan (1991) *The Versailles Settlement: Peacemaking in Paris.* London. A good survey.

Siklos, P. L. (1995) 'Hyperinflations: their origins, development and termination. In Siklos, P. L. (ed.) *Great Inflations of the Twentieth Century: Theories, Policies and Evidence.* pp. 3–34. Aldershot. An excellently readable survey.

Soutou, G.-H. (1998) The French peacemakers and their home front. In Boemecke, M. F., Feldman, G. D., Glaser, E. (eds.) *The Treaty of Versailles. A Reassessment after 75 Years.* pp. 167–88. Cambridge.

Spoerer, M. (1996) *Vom Scheingewinn zum Rüstungsboom. Die Eigenkapitalrentabilität der deutschen Industrieaktiengesellschaften 1925–41.* Stuttgart. A groundbreaking study of German interwar profitability.

Stachura, P. (ed.) (1986), *Unemployment and the Great Depression in Weimar Germany.* London. On the social aspects.

Stocking, G. H. and Watkins, M. (1947) *Cartels in Action. Case Studies in International Business Diplomacy.* New York.

Stollberg, G. (1981) *Die Rationalisierungsdebatte, 1908–1933. Freie Gewerkschaften zwischen Mitwirkung und Gegenwehr.* Frankfurt/Main. Discusses the trade union attitudes to rationalisation.

Taussig, F. W. (1920) Germany's Reparations payments. *American Economic Review, Papers and Proceedings of the Thirty-Second Annual Meeting of the AEA,* pp. 33–49. An optimistic neoclassical view of reparations payments.

Temin, P. (1971) The beginning of the Depression in Germany. *Economic History Review,* 24, 240–48. A denial that the Wall Street boom caused the German slump.

Tilly, R. and Huck, N. 1994, Die deutsche Wirtschaft in der Krise, 1929 bis 1934. Ein makroökonomischer Ansatz. In Buchheim, C., Hutter, M., James, H. (eds.) *Zerrissene Zwischenkriegszeit: Wirtschaftshistorische*

*Beiträge. Knut Borchardt zum 65 Geburtstag.* pp. 45–95. Baden-Baden. A detailed Keynesian analysis of the German slump.

Tooze, J. A. (1999) Weimar's statistical economics: Ernst Wagemann, the Reich's Statistical Office and the Institute for Business Cycle Research 1925–33. *Economic History Review*, 52, 523–42.

Trachtenberg, M. (1980) *Reparation in World Politics: France and European Economic Diplomacy 1916–1923.* New York. Argues the rationality and moderation of French reparations policy.

The Treaties of Peace (1924) *Vol. I: Containing the Treaty of Versailles, the Treaty of St. Germain and the Treaty of Trianon.* New York.

Tschirbs, R. (1982) Der Ruhrbergmann zwischen Priviligierung und Statusverlust: Lohnpolitik von der Inflation bis zur Rationalisierung. In Feldman, G. D., Holtfrerich, C.-L., Ritter, G. A., Witt, P. C. (eds.) *The German Inflation Reconsidered. A Preliminary Balance.* pp. 308–46. Berlin.

Voth, H. J. (1995) Did high wages or high interest rates bring down the Weimar Republic? *Journal of Economic History*, 55, 801–21. Argues for high interest rates.

   (2000) German banking and the impact of the First World War. In Wrigley, C. (ed.) *The First World War and the International Economy.* Cheltenham.

   (Forthcoming) With a bang, not a whimper: pricking Germany's 'stock-market bubble' in 1927 and the slide into depression. *Journal of Economic History.*

Warriner, D. (1931) *Combines and Rationalisation in Germany.* London. A good contemporary description.

Webb S. B. (1986) Fiscal news and inflationary expectations in Germany. *Journal of Economic History*, 46, 769–94.

   (1988) Latin American debt today and German reparations after World War I – a comparison. *Weltwirtschaftliches Archiv*, 124, 745–74.

   (1989) *Hyperinflation and Stabilization in Weimar Germany.* Oxford. Major monograph on the inflation emphasising the role of reparations expectations.

Weisbrod, B. (1990) Industrial crisis strategy in the Great Depression. In Kruedener, J. Freiherr von (ed.) *Economic Crisis and Political Collapse: The Weimar Republic 1924–1933.* pp. 45–62. New York. Argues that business 'instrumentalised' the Depression.

Williams, J. H. (1921–2) German foreign trade and reparations payments. *Quarterly Journal of Economics*, 36, 482–503.

Witt, P.-C. (1979) Inflation, Wohnungszwangswirtschaft und Hauszinssteuer. Zur Regelung von Wohnungsbau und Wohnungsmarkt in der Weimarer Republik. In Niethammer, L. (ed.) *Wohnen im Wandel. Beiträge zur Geschichte des Alltags in der bürgerlichen Gesellschaft.* pp. 385–407. Wuppertal. An excellent account of housing policy during the Republic.

(1982a) Finanzpolitik als Verfassungs- und Gesellschaftspolitik. Überlegungen zur Finanzpolitik des Deutschen Reiches in den Jahren 1930 bis 1932. *Geschichte und Gesellschaft*, 8, 387–414. A political economy of fiscal policy in the slump.

(1982b) Staatliche Wirtschaftspolitik in Deutschland 1918–1920: Entwicklung und Zerstörung einer modernen wirtschaftspolitischen Strategie. In Feldman, G. D., Holtfrerich, C.-L., Ritter, G. A., Witt, P. C. (eds.) *The German Inflation Reconsidered: A Preliminary Balance.* pp. 151–79. Berlin. The thesis that German policy in 1918–19 was an incipiently Keynesian stabilisation policy.

(1983) Tax policies, tax assessment and inflation. Toward a sociology of the public finances in the German inflation 1914–1923. In Schmukler, N. and Marcus, E. (eds.) *Inflation through the Ages: Economic, Social, Psychological and Historical Aspects.* pp. 450–72. New York.

# Index